ECDL® Advanced 2.0

European Computer Driving Licence

Module AM4 - Spreadsheets

Using Microsoft® Excel 2010

Release ECDL271v1

Published by:

        CiA Training Ltd
        Business & Innovation Centre
        Sunderland Enterprise Park
        Sunderland
        SR5 2TA
        United Kingdom

        Tel: +44 (0) 191 549 5002
        Fax: +44 (0) 191 549 9005

        E-mail: info@ciatraining.co.uk
        Web: www.ciatraining.co.uk

        ISBN: 978-1-86005-850-9

Important Note

This guide was written for *Microsoft Office 2010* running on *Windows 7*. If using earlier versions of *Windows* some dialog boxes may look and function slightly differently to that described.

A screen resolution of *1024x768* is assumed. Working at a different resolution (or with an application window which is not maximised) may change the look of the dynamic *Office 2010 Ribbon*, which changes to fit the space available.

For example, the **Editing Group** on a full *Ribbon* will contain several buttons, but if space is restricted it may be replaced by an **Editing Button** (which, when clicked, will display the full **Editing Group**).

First published 2010

European Computer Driving Licence, ECDL, International Computer Driving Licence, ICDL, e-Citizen and related logos are all registered Trade Marks of The European Computer Driving Licence Foundation Limited ("ECDL Foundation").

CiA Training Ltd is an entity independent of ECDL Foundation and is not associated with ECDL Foundation in any manner. This courseware may be used to assist candidates to prepare for the ECDL Foundation Certification Programme as titled on the courseware. Neither ECDL Foundation nor **CiA Training Ltd** warrants that the use of this courseware publication will ensure passing of the tests for that ECDL Foundation Certification Programme. This courseware publication has been independently reviewed and approved by ECDL Foundation as covering the learning objectives for the ECDL Foundation Certification Programme.

Confirmation of this approval can be obtained by viewing the relevant ECDL Foundation Certification Programme training material page of the website www.ecdl.org.

The material contained in this courseware publication has not been reviewed for technical accuracy and does not guarantee that candidates will pass the test for the ECDL Foundation Certification Programme. Any and all assessment items and/or performance-based exercises contained in this courseware relate solely to this publication and do not constitute or imply certification by ECDL Foundation in respect of the ECDL Foundation Certification Programme or any other ECDL Foundation test. Irrespective of how the material contained in this courseware is deployed, for example in a learning management system (LMS) or a customised interface, nothing should suggest to the candidate that this material constitutes certification or can lead to certification through any other process than official ECDL Foundation certification testing.

For details on sitting a test for an ECDL Foundation certification programme, please contact your country's designated National Licensee or visit the ECDL Foundation's website at www.ecdl.org.

Candidates using this courseware must be registered with the National Operator before undertaking a test for an ECDL Foundation Certification Programme. Without a valid registration, the test(s) cannot be undertaken and no certificate, nor any other form of recognition, can be given to a candidate. Registration should be undertaken with your country's designated National Licensee at an Approved Test Centre.

Downloading the Data Files

The data files associated with these exercises must be downloaded from our website. Go to *www.ciatraining.co.uk/data* and follow the on screen instructions to download the appropriate data files.

By default, the data files will be installed to **CIA DATA FILES \ Advanced ECDL \ AM4 Excel 2010 Data** in your **Documents** library\folder (or **My Documents** in *Windows XP*).

If you prefer, the data can be supplied on CD at an additional cost. Contact the Sales team at *info@ciatraining.co.uk*.

Aims

To provide the student with an understanding of the more advanced concepts of spreadsheet models using Excel.

Objectives

After completing the guide the user will be able to:

- Create and maintain complex spreadsheets
- Manipulate charts
- Create and use Scenarios
- Create and use Templates
- Link cells, worksheets and workbooks
- Use complicated Functions of various types
- Use Data Tables and Databases
- Create and use simple Macros
- Use Auditing techniques to check for errors

Assessment of Knowledge

At the end of this guide is a section called the **Record of Achievement Matrix**. Before the guide is started it is recommended that the user complete the matrix to measure the level of current knowledge.

Tick boxes are provided for each feature. **1** is for no knowledge, **2** some knowledge and **3** is for competent.

After working through a section, complete the **Record of Achievement Matrix** for that section and only when competent in all areas move on to the next section.

Contents

Section 1
Introduction

By the end of this Section you should be able to:

Understand Spreadsheet Design

Identify the Different Techniques to Use

To gain an understanding of the above features, work through the **Driving Lessons** in this **Section**.

For each **Driving Lesson**, read the **Park and Read** instructions, without touching the keyboard, then work through the numbered steps of the **Manoeuvres** on the computer. Complete the **Revision Exercise(s)** at the end of the section to test your knowledge.

Driving Lesson 1 - Spreadsheet Design

🅿 Park and Read

Whilst any course on advanced spreadsheet applications needs to describe and explain the techniques necessary to produce successful worksheets, thought should always be given to the overall purpose of the finished spreadsheet and to the intended users.

Structure

Excel supports multi-sheet workbooks. A saved spreadsheet file is called a workbook. Each workbook can contain a vast number of worksheets. Each worksheet is a spreadsheet. Information can be passed from sheet to sheet, enabling large complicated models to be created using simpler smaller parts. For a company this is invaluable, different members of staff can provide data that feeds into a bigger picture worksheet, one where all the totals can be collected without the minute detail.

Purpose

Every worksheet produced has a purpose. Before starting to create a worksheet, take some time to consider the purpose behind it, how it will be used and the results that it needs to present, then plan the design accordingly.

Example 1. You are creating a spreadsheet to input and display departmental budgets and consolidate them into an overall company budget. Will each department complete its own piece of the worksheet, or will it be more efficient to have separate worksheets for each department and join them together later as a separate process? Will the results need to be incorporated into a larger financial report, in which case the formatting and structure will need to be compatible?

Example 2. You are creating a spreadsheet to record membership details for a club or gym. You need to know what the list will be used for. Does it need to record payment of fees? Will it be used to analyse membership over various activities or groups? If so, relevant details need to be included. Will it be used to send out letters to members? If so, it will need to include names and addresses.

Example 3. You are creating a spreadsheet to present statistical viewing figures for a television channel. Does it need to show a series of charts without the original data, or just the data so that users can create their own charts? What analysis will be required? If it needs to be analysed by region for example, then regional information must be included with the original data.

continued over

Driving Lesson 1 - Continued

Audience

The intended users of your spreadsheet have a major impact on the way it is designed in two areas.

Firstly in the way it is presented. A company financial report for the Financial Director may need to have summary information analysed by various factors, using pivot tables and charts for example. The same data for an accountant or auditor may need to see the detailed breakdown of all totals into the individual items that make them up.

Secondly, many practical spreadsheets are dynamic, i.e. they will require frequent updating, and so users will be using your spreadsheet for data input and manipulation. Are your users going to merely read the data you give them, or are they expecting to analyse it themselves using filters and sorts for example. Make sure your design takes into account the competence of the people who will be doing this.

Other Considerations

There are often practical considerations to spreadsheet design. A working spreadsheet can in principle be as large as you like, but scrolling horizontally and vertically in a spreadsheet can become confusing. Try to arrange the layout so that scrolling is only necessary in one direction, or it may be better to split the solution into several linked worksheets where possible.

The final form of your spreadsheet may also affect its style. You may be asked to produce a spreadsheet that will be used on a web page or presentation slide. This will require that the final result is compact enough for this purpose.

Driving Lesson 2 - Techniques to Use

🅿 Park and Read

Spreadsheet software such as *Microsoft Excel* enables you to produce professional looking, functional worksheets for many different purposes. No matter what type of job you do, it's likely that at some stage you will need a list or table of data that requires some kind of manipulation or numerical processing, e.g. sorting, filtering or totalling and a spreadsheet would be the best solution for such a task.

In particular, *Excel* has many features that allow you to create complex spreadsheets, i.e. multi page sheets containing a variety of formatting styles and techniques and possibly containing various analysis and graphical presentation. Some of the relevant skills and techniques are:

- **Advanced editing and formatting**. Including custom and conditional formatting, hiding selected data and using subtotalling.

- **Templates**. Allowing many worksheets to be based on the same consistent style.

- **Security**. Restricting access to spreadsheets or protecting the content of certain cells within spreadsheets.

- **Linking**. Links to data within worksheets, between worksheets and between different workbooks.

- **Lists**. The specific features which can be used when the spreadsheet is in a list format.

- **Sorting**. Including custom sorts.

- **Querying/Filtering**. Including advanced filtering options.

- **Charts and Graphs**. Including formatting and modifying of various chart types.

- **Functions**. Using a wide range of functions, including numerical, text, logical and lookup. Also includes complex formulas with nested functions.

- **Analysis techniques**. Including pivot tables, scenarios, and data tables.

- **Auditing**. Including error tracing, formula display and working with comments.

- **Macros**. Instructions to perform repetitive tasks with a single command.

- **Links**. To allow users of the documentation to access relevant data from other sources.

- **Hyperlink**. Text that when clicked takes the user to another source, i.e. opens a different workbook, word document, etc.

Driving Lesson 3 - Revision: Introduction

This is not an ECDL test. Testing may only be carried out through certified ECDL test centres. This covers the features introduced in this section. Try not to refer to the preceding Driving Lessons while completing it.

1.   When designing a spreadsheet, what are the advantages of splitting a large task into several smaller tasks using different worksheets/workbooks?

2.   When designing a large spreadsheet why should it either fit horizontally or vertically on the screen, if possible?

3.   When creating a spreadsheet for others why is protection of the data so important?

4.   After creating a spreadsheet for others to use, what other tasks may you be required to do?

5.   If you were a designer and seller of kitchens or bathrooms, what techniques might you use when creating supporting spreadsheets?

6.   What is a template?

7.   What is a macro?

8.   If you were charged with assembling the sales figures for a company, how would you present them?

9.   What is the difference between a link and a hyperlink?

 *Answers are shown in the **Answers** section at the end of the guide.*

If you experienced any difficulty completing this Revision refer back to the Driving Lessons in this section. Then redo the Revision.

Once you are confident with the features, complete the Record of Achievement Matrix referring to the section at the end of the guide. Only when competent move on to the next Section.

Section 2
Formatting

By the end of this Section you should be able to:

Split Windows

Use Conditional Formatting

Use Format as a Table

Use Paste Special

Transpose Data

Copy and Move Sheets

To gain an understanding of the above features, work through the **Driving Lessons** in this **Section**.

For each **Driving Lesson**, read the **Park and Read** instructions, without touching the keyboard, then work through the numbered steps of the **Manoeuvres** on the computer. Complete the **Revision Exercise(s)** at the end of the section to test your knowledge.

Driving Lesson 4 - Split a Window

▣ Park and Read

Split is similar to freeze panes except that the individual panes can be scrolled to show different information in each pane.

↱ Manoeuvres

1. Open the workbook **Retail** (see page 4 - **Downloading the Data Files** for the location).

2. **Split** is created at the active cell position using the **Ribbon**. Click on cell **F8**. Display the **View** tab and then click the **Split** button ⊞ Split , in the **Window** group. The worksheet is now split into four areas, all displaying the same worksheet.

3. Move the active cell to the right and up a few cells, using the arrow keys.

4. Use the four scroll bars to display different parts of the worksheet to create four different views of the same worksheet - very useful if using a large worksheet.

5. The split can be moved by clicking on the split lines and dragging them when ╬ appears. Drag the vertical split to the left to display only 2 columns in the left panes.

6. To remove the **Split,** click the **Split** button again.

7. **Split** can also be created using the split boxes at the top or right of the **Scroll Bars**.

8. Drag the **Horizontal Split** button at the top of the vertical scroll bar down to between rows **7** and **8**. Drag the **Vertical Split** button at the right of the horizontal scroll bar down to between columns **E** and **F**. This achieves the same split as created using the **Ribbon**.

9. An alternative method to remove a single split is to double click on the split line or the split box. Remove the horizontal and then the vertical split.

10. Leave the workbook **Retail** open for the next Driving Lesson.

Driving Lesson 5 - Conditional Formatting

🅿 Park and Read

As well as applying formatting to certain cells, it is possible to apply different formatting to cells depending on the values within those cells. Selected cells can be compared to a value, or the results of a formula, to decide which format should be used. This is called **Conditional Formatting**.

Multiple conditions can be used to determine the formatting for the same cell, so for example, a cell could be coloured red if it is below a certain value and blue if it is greater than another value.

𝄢 Manoeuvres

1.   Open the workbook **Retail**, if it is not already open.

2.   Highlight the **Turnover** figures, the range **B4:M4**.

3.   With the **Home** tab displayed, from the **Styles** group, select **Conditional Formatting**.

4.   Select **New Rule**. The **New Formatting Rule** dialog box is displayed.

5.   From the **Select a Rule Type** box click on **Format only cells that contain**.

6.   In the drop down criteria box (**between**) select **less than or equal to**.

7.   Enter the value **19000** in the next box.

continued over

Driving Lesson 5 - Continued

i   *If entering a formula in the value box remember to start with =*

8. Click the **Format** button and select the font colour **red**. Click **OK**. Click **OK** again to apply the rule.

9. To add another condition to the same range, click the **Conditional Formatting** icon and select **New Rule**. Select **Format only cells that contain**, again. Select **greater than** and enter **25000** in the next box. Format the text to be **bold** and **blue**. Click **OK** and **OK** again to apply the formatting.

10. Highlight the range **B14:M14**, apply the conditional formatting, values **less than** the average of the range **=Average($B$14:$M$14)**. Format the range with a **pale yellow** cell shading using the **Fill** tab and **More Colors** option. Click **OK, OK** and **OK** again.

11. To remove **Conditional Formatting**, select the range **B4:M4**, click **Conditional Formatting** and select **Manage Rules**.

i   *The current selection has two rules applied to it. To view all the rules, select **This Worksheet** from the **Show formatting rules for** box.*

12. Select the **Cell Value > 25000** rule and click the **Delete Rule** button, ✗ Delete Rule. Click **OK**. All values of over **25000** should now not be **blue** or **bold**.

13. Experiment with adding and removing conditional formats to highlight results in a way that had not been possible before.

14. Close the workbook <u>without</u> saving.

Driving Lesson 6 - Format as Table

🅿 Park and Read

There is a set of pre-defined worksheet formats to enhance the appearance of a worksheet, via the **Home** tab **Styles** group, **Format as Table** command.

🏁 Manoeuvres

1. Open the workbook **Budget**.

2. Highlight the range **A1:N14** and on the **Home** tab, in the **Styles** group, click **Format as Table**.

3. There is a list of the available **Table Formats**, covering **Light, Medium** and **Dark** options. Scroll through the list of **Table Formats**. Select **Table Style Light 2**.

4. Click **OK** to confirm the range that is to be formatted.

5. The sheet is now formatted in the **Light 2** style. A **Design** tab is displayed on the ribbon, showing various groups for different types of formatting.

6. To change the table format, select an option from the **Table Styles** group on the **Design** tab. Click the **More** drop down (shown below) to display all the available styles. The sheet displays each format as the mouse passes over it.

More

7. To remove the table format, with the range **A1:N14** selected, click the **More** button in the **Table Styles** group on the **Design** tab and then select **Clear**.

8. With a filled cell selected, display the **Data** tab and click the **Filter** button to clear the filter buttons.

9. Close the workbook <u>without</u> saving.

Driving Lesson 7 - Paste Special

🅿 Park and Read

When using **Copy** and **Paste** or **Cut** and **Paste**, the default is to paste the cell exactly as it was originally. **Paste Special** is used to paste cell information when a complete copy is not required. For example, **Paste Special** can:

- Paste only formulas, values or formats. Pasting values from cells that contain formulas is a way of fixing the data, as it will never then be recalculated.
- Combine ranges using an operation, e.g. adding, subtracting, etc.
- Transpose ranges (change a spreadsheet round by converting rows to columns and columns to rows).
- Paste links to the original data (covered in a later section).

Manoeuvres

1. Open the workbook **Finances**.

2. Highlight the range **A1:N1**. Change the range to italic and the font colour to **blue**.

3. To paste this formatting to another range, click the cell **A1** and in the **Home** tab, **Clipboard** group, click the **Copy** button.

4. Highlight the range **A2:A16** and select the **Paste** drop down arrow.

5. Many paste options are displayed in the drop down panel, but for the purposes of this exercise, select **Paste Special** to display the **Paste Special** dialog box.

6. Under **Paste** select the **Formats** option and click **OK** to paste the formatting. The cell border from **A1** is pasted as well. Remove the unwanted borders to match those in column **B**.

continued over

Driving Lesson 7 - Continued

7.   Open the workbook **Outgoings**.

8.   Select the range **A1:L10** and click on the **Copy** button.

9.   Click on the *Excel* button on the **Taskbar** and then select the **Finances** workbook to make it active.

10.   Click on cell **B5**. Click the **Paste** button to paste the contents normally.

11.   Data can be pasted using a mathematical operation. Open the file **Income** and highlight the range **A1:L2**, the income figures.

12.   Click the **Copy** button.

13.   Switch back to **Finances** using the **Taskbar**.

14.   The income figures are to go into the range **B2:M3** but this range already contains data, which would be overwritten if a normal paste was used. To keep the original data, select cell **B2** then click the **Paste** drop down and select **Paste Special**.

15.   Under **Operation** click **Add** to add the two sets of figures together, then click **OK**. The data is now combined.

i *The **Add** operation was used in this example. **Subtract**, **Multiply** and **Divide** work in the same way.*

16.   It may be required to convert formulas to values because the numbers are final, e.g. a VAT return or expenditure after the month end, etc. Using the **Finances** workbook, January has ended and the figures in column B are required to be converted to values. Check the cells **B4**, **B15** and **B16** to see that they contain formulas.

17.   Select the range **B2:B16**.

18.   Click **Copy**, then click the **Paste** drop down and select **Paste Special**.

19.   Under **Paste**, select the **Values** option and click **OK**. Click away from the selection.

20.   Check that the cells **B4**, **B15** and **B16** contain values.

i *Remember that this process removes formulas and therefore the worksheet cannot be used again. If repeated use is required, create and use a template.*

21.   Save the workbook as **Finances2** and close it.

22.   Close the workbooks **Income** and **Outgoings** <u>without</u> saving.

Driving Lesson 8 - Transposing Data

▣ Park and Read

It is sometimes necessary to change the way data is stored in a worksheet. Data stored in rows may be needed in columns and vice versa. This process is called **Transposing Data**.

↱ Manoeuvres

1.   Open the workbook **Transpose**. The **Result** column is needed in a row.

2.   Select the range **B3:C17**, then select to **Copy** the range.

3.   Move to **A20** and click the **Paste** drop down and select **Paste Special**. Check the **Transpose** box.

4.   Click **OK**. Press **<Esc>** to exit the copy command.

5.   The data is now shown in rows. Notice that the formats, i.e. the borders, have also been copied. This could have been avoided by selecting to paste just **Values** in the **Paste Special** dialog box.

6.   Transpose the range **B3:C17**, with values only, to **A23**.

7.   Close the workbook <u>without</u> saving.

8.   Open the workbook **Budget**.

9.   Transpose the range **A1:N14** to cell **A18**.

10. The borders are not appropriate. Undo the paste and transpose the range again, this time pasting only values.

11. Highlight the new range and add new borders as appropriate.

12. Check the formulas and print a landscape copy of the worksheet on one page.

13. Close the workbook <u>without</u> saving.

Driving Lesson 9 - Copying and Moving Sheets

🅿 Park and Read

Sheets within a workbook can be moved or copied within the same workbook or to a different workbook.

👣 Manoeuvres

1. Open the workbook **Divisions**.

2. Sheets can be moved and copied within the same workbook by dragging the sheet tab with the mouse. Move the **North Midlands** sheet to between **South Wales** and **Midlands** by clicking and dragging the tab to the correct position (the black triangle always shows where the sheet will be inserted). More sheets will appear when the cursor reaches the end of the displayed sheets.

3. Move the **North West** sheet to between **North** and **North East**.

> ℹ️ *Use the **Sheet navigation** buttons to locate the sheets that are not visible.*

4. A sheet is copied within the same workbook by holding <Ctrl> while dragging the sheet tab. To make a copy of the **North** sheet, hold down <Ctrl> and click and drag the **North** sheet tab across to the right, next to **North**. Release the mouse button first before <Ctrl>.

> ℹ️ *The name of the copied sheet is **North (2)**. Duplicate sheet names are not allowed. A sheet is renamed by double clicking on it and entering a new name.*

5. If a sheet is to be moved or copied to another workbook the shortcut menu is used. Right click on the **North (2)** sheet tab.

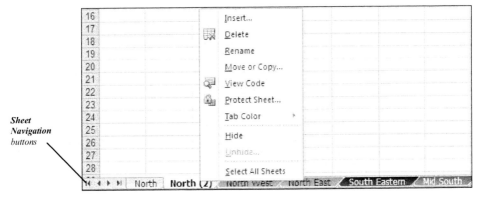

6. This menu controls all the actions relating to sheets. Select **Move or Copy**.

continued over

Driving Lesson 9 - Continued

   *This above dialog box can also be displayed by using the **Home** tab, **Cells** group, **Format** button then under **Organize Sheets**, **Move or Copy Sheets**.*

7. To create a copy the **Create a copy** box is checked, otherwise the sheet is moved. Check the **Create a copy** box.

8. To move or copy to a different workbook, select from the **To book** box. Drop down the list and select **(new book)**.

   *To move or copy to an existing workbook it must already be open, so it is displayed in the **To book** box.*

9. The **Before sheet** box is empty for a new workbook. An existing one would display all the sheets for a selection to be made on the placement. Click **OK**.

10. A new workbook is started with just the sheet **North (2)** in it. Display the **Divisions** workbook and check that **North (2)** is still in this book and that it was copied.

11. Close both workbooks <u>without</u> saving.

Driving Lesson 10 - Revision: Formatting

This is not an ECDL test. Testing may only be carried out through certified ECDL test centres. This covers the features introduced in this section. Try not to refer to the preceding Driving Lessons while completing it.

1.　　Open the workbook **House**.

2.　　Format the range **B2:N16** as currency with two decimal places.

3.　　Freeze the column and row titles.

4.　　Scroll off the screen to check that the titles are frozen.

5.　　Format the whole worksheet in **Table Style Medium 3**.

6.　　The screen is cluttered, change the row height of rows **2** to **16** to **15.00** units (20 pixels).

7.　　The screen is now cluttered with zeros, reformat the range **B2:N16** as **Currency** with no decimal places, to remove some of them.

8.　　Apply conditional formatting to the range **B16:N16** the accumulated savings row, to display amounts greater than **1000** to be bold and displayed in blue text and saving levels under **0** in bold and displayed in red text.

9.　　An unexpected windfall comes in the form of a **£500** pay bonus in **February**. Make the necessary change. Note the effects of the conditional formatting on row **16**.

10.　Highlight the range **A1:N16** and using paste special make a copy on a new sheet, but paste only the values.

11.　Check the cells in rows **4**, **15** and **16** that contained formulas but are now just numbers. Change cell **B2** to **0**. It has no impact on any other cells.

12.　Save the workbook as **House2**.

13.　Close the workbook.

If you experienced any difficulty completing this Revision refer back to the Driving Lessons in this section. Then redo the Revision.

Once you are confident with the features, complete the Record of Achievement Matrix referring to the section at the end of the guide. Only when competent move on to the next Section.

Section 3
Protection

By the end of this Section you should be able to:

Protect Cells

Hide and Unhide Columns and Rows

Create Read-Only Workbooks

Hide and Unhide Worksheets and Workbooks

Protect Workbooks

Hide Formulas

To gain an understanding of the above features, work through the **Driving Lessons** in this **Section**.

For each **Driving Lesson**, read the **Park and Read** instructions, without touching the keyboard, then work through the numbered steps of the **Manoeuvres** on the computer. Complete the **Revision Exercise(s)** at the end of the section to test your knowledge.

Driving Lesson 11 - Protection

▣ Park and Read

Varying levels of protection can be applied to workbooks, individual worksheets and cells within worksheets. Opening sensitive files or data can be controlled by using passwords, either by preventing access completely or allowing files to be examined but not amended (Read Only access).

Specific areas within spreadsheets can be protected from accidental or deliberate alteration, by applying cell locking.

The following protection is available:

Passwords   prevent the workbooks from being opened by unauthorised users.

Cell Locking   prevents important cell data (usually formulas) from being amended or deleted. Cell locking is only activated when worksheet protection is switched on.

Workbooks   can have passwords added to them. They can be made **Read Only** to prevent changes.

Worksheets   can have cells locked to prevent changes and optionally, a password added to protect locked data and worksheet structure. A protected worksheet can only have data entered into unlocked cells and formatting cannot be carried out. When worksheet protection is disabled (the default) all cells are accessible whether locked or not.

Driving Lesson 12 - Worksheet & Cell Protection

▣ Park and Read

Worksheets can be protected with passwords so that no changes can be made to the locked cells within them.

By default all cells on a worksheet are locked, but this has no effect until worksheet protection is activated.

To allow changes to be made to some cells but not others when the worksheet is protected, it is necessary to unlock the editable cells, prior to adding the protection. This is often used when providing a spreadsheet for other users for data entry. All titles and formulas are locked to prevent changes, and only the cells where data is to be entered are unlocked and therefore accessible.

☞ Manoeuvres

1.   Open the workbook **Invoices**.

2.   To protect the worksheet from changes, from the **Home** tab, **Cells** group, select **Format** then click **Protect Sheet**.

ℹ️ *An alternative method to display this dialog box is to display the **File** tab, select the **Info** option, click the **Protect Workbook** button and select **Protect Current Sheet**.*

3.   Entering a password is optional (be careful when using passwords as access to protected worksheets is prohibited without the password). Type **pass**. The password appears as ******** it is not displayed on the screen. Click **OK**.

ℹ️ *Passwords are case sensitive.*

continued over

Driving Lesson 12 - Continued

4.   Confirm the password by typing **pass** again. Click **OK**.

5.   Click on any cell and try to enter some data. No changes can be made to any cell on the worksheet. *Excel* displays the following message.

6.   Click **OK**.

7.   To remove the protection, display the **Format** drop down list and select **Unprotect Sheet**. Enter the password **pass** and click **OK** to remove the worksheet protection.

8.   To allow changes to cells on a protected sheet, the required cells must first be **unlocked**. Select the range **E6:E14**. These are the cells that may be changed after protection has been added.

9.   Display the **Format** drop down list and click **Lock Cell**. The protection of the range is now unlocked.

10.   Having unlocked the required cells, to take effect, the worksheet has to be protected. Re-protect the sheet.

*Remember that a password is optional and can be omitted, but the protection can then be removed by using the **Unprotect Sheet** command.*

11.   Enter the password **pass** and click **OK**.

12.   Confirm the password by typing **pass** again. Click **OK**.

13.   Move to **E7** and change the contents to **£1500.00**.

14.   Move to **F7** and try to change the **VAT** to **£250**. This cell is locked. Only the **Amount** column may be changed, i.e. the range **E6:E14**, that was unlocked previously. Click **OK**.

15.   Change cell **E10** to **750**. This is allowed as the cell is unlocked.

16.   Close the workbook **Invoices** <u>without</u> saving the changes.

Driving Lesson 13 - Hiding Rows & Columns

▣ Park and Read

Rows and/or **Columns** of sensitive data can be hidden from view. The data in any hidden rows and columns is still included in calculations, so that the results of the sheet are unaffected.

↷ Manoeuvres

1. Open the workbook **Budget**.

2. Highlight the rows **5** and **6**. From the **Home** tab, **Cells** group, display the **Format** drop down list select **Hide & Unhide** then **Hide Rows**. Rows 5 and 6 have now been hidden.

	A	B	C	D	E	F
1	Budget	Jan	Feb	Mar	Apr	May
2	Sales	6000	6400	7200	6200	5300
3	Price	6	6	6	6	6
4	Turnover	36000	38400	43200	37200	31800
7	Wages	6400	6400	6400	6400	6400
8	Materials	20800	22400	25600	21600	18000
9	Overheads	5000	5000	5000	5000	5000

Rows 5 and 6 are hidden. Note that row 7 still calculates Wages.

3. To re-display rows **5** and **6**, highlight a range in row **4** to row **7**, e.g. **A4:A7** and from the **Format** drop down list select **Hide & Unhide** then **Unhide Rows**.

4. A column can be hidden in a similar way, but another method is to use the shortcut menu. Right click on the column heading **F** and select **Hide** from the shortcut menu.

5. To re-display column **F**, select columns **E** to **G**, right click and select **Unhide**.

6. Columns and rows may also be hidden by dragging their borders until the column width or the row height is zero. To hide column **M** using this method, place the mouse pointer on the column divider between **M** and **N**. Drag the adjust cursor to the left, carefully, until the column width is **0.00**.

ℹ *Dragging further left hides multiple columns. If this happens, use **Undo** to restore the columns and try again.*

7. The mouse can also be used to unhide columns or rows. There are two adjust cursors. The normal column adjust cursor is on the left or for a row is above. To the right of a hidden column or below a hidden row the adjust cursor changes to ◀║▶ or ▲/▼. Dragging this cursor redisplays the hidden data. Unhide column **M** making it **10.00 (75 pixels)** wide.

8. Close the workbook <u>without</u> saving.

Driving Lesson 14 - Hiding Formulas

🅿 Park and Read

The **Hidden** option on the **Protection** tab of the **Format Cells** dialog box prevents a cell's contents from being displayed in the **Formula Bar** and is used primarily to hide source formulas (how the results were calculated). The cell contents still display the results.

🄵 Manoeuvres

1. Open the workbook **Invoices** and select the range **F6:F14**.

2. On the **Home** tab, click **Format** in the **Cells** group and select **Format Cells**. In the dialog box display the **Protection** tab. Check **Hidden**, then click **OK**.

3. Click **Format** in the **Cells** group, select **Protect Sheet**, click **OK** to turn on the sheet protection <u>without</u> a password.

4. Move the cell pointer into cell **F6**. Notice that the result value is displayed in the cell but the content (formula) is not shown in the **Formula Bar**. **Hidden** prevents the **Formulas** from being viewed even if the resulting values are displayed on the sheet.

Formula Bar blank

	F6	▼		fx			
◢	A	B	C	D	E	F	G
1							
2							
3							
4							
5	Invoice	Date	Co. No.	Company	Amount	VAT	Total
6	156	3-Dec-06	378	Greens	£456.00	£79.80	£535.80
7	164	15-Dec-06	294	Smith & Co	£900.00	£157.50	£1,057.50
8	167	21-Dec-06	345	J Jones	£1,345.00	£235.38	£1,580.38

ℹ️ *Hidden data only hides content from the **Formula Bar**. If it is required to completely hide values in individual cells then change the font colour to match the background colour or hide the whole row/column. This must be done before the worksheet is protected.*

5. To display the formulas again, click **Format** in the **Cells** group and click **Unprotect Sheet** to turn off the sheet protection.

6. Highlight the range **F6:F14**, click **Format** in the **Cells** group, then **Format Cells** and display the **Protection** tab. Uncheck **Hidden**, then click **OK**.

7. Click on individual cells in the range **F6:F14** and check that the formulas are displayed in the **Formula Bar**.

8. Close the workbook **Invoices** <u>without</u> saving.

Driving Lesson 15 - Workbook Protection

▣ Park and Read

Workbooks may contain sensitive or private data which means that the whole workbook has to be kept secure. **Passwords** can be assigned to workbooks so that only those people who know the password can open them.

🗺 Manoeuvres

1. Open the workbook **Retail**.

2. Click the **File** tab then select **Save As**. From the **Save As** dialog box click the **Tools** button and select **General Options**.

3. In the **Password to open** box, type **PASS** (passwords are case-sensitive. **PASS** is not the same as **pass** or **Pass**). Note that the letters do not appear as you type, only asterisks. Click **OK**.

ℹ️ *Choose a password that is easily remembered, but not so obvious that it can be easily guessed. If passwords are forgotten, the workbook cannot be opened, so the data within all the sheets is lost!*

4. To confirm the password, it must be re-entered. Enter it, then click **OK**.

5. In the **Save As** dialog box, enter **Secure** in the **File name** box, then click **Save**.

6. Close the workbook **Secure** and open it again. A prompt for the password will be displayed.

continued over

Driving Lesson 15 - Continued

7.   Try typing in an **Incorrect** password and clicking **OK**. Access is denied.

8.   Open the workbook **Secure**, this time enter the correct password, **PASS**. Click **OK**.

9.   Workbooks can also be saved with a password to modify added. **Password to modify** allows users who know the password to open, edit and save as normal. Click the **File** tab then select **Save As**. From the **Save As** dialog box click the **Tools** button and select **General Options**.

10. Remove the asterisks from the **Password to open** box and then enter the password **change** in the **Password to modify** box. Click **OK**.

11. Re-enter the password **change** and click **OK**.

12. Click **Save** and then **Yes** to overwrite the previously saved workbook.

13. Close the workbook **Secure**.

14. Users without the password to modify can still open the workbook but as **Read-only**. Any changes made in the workbook mean it has to be saved with a new name, keeping the original unchanged. Open the workbook **Secure**.

15. The user has a choice to enter the password and proceed normally or as stated, to click the **Read Only** button. Enter the password **change** and click **OK**. The workbook opens with full editing rights.

16. Make a change to any cell in the workbook, save it and then close it.

17. Open the workbook **Secure** and on this occasion click the **Read Only** button. The workbook opens as a read only document. Make a change to the workbook and try and save it with the same name. Click **OK** at the message and then **Cancel** to close the dialog box. Close the workbook <u>without</u> saving the change.

18. Open the workbook **Secure** again, enter the password **change** and click **OK**. To remove the password protection, click the **File** tab, then **Save As**. Click the **Tools** button and then select **General Options**. Delete the asterisks in the **Password to modify** box, click **OK** and save the file under the same name, replacing the existing workbook.

19. Close the workbook.

Driving Lesson 16 - Hiding Worksheets & Workbooks

▣ Park and Read

A workbook or a worksheet can be hidden, when the contents are needed but are not to be seen. Hidden worksheets and the workbook still remain open.

☞ Manoeuvres

1. Open the workbooks **Spires** and **Budget**.

2. With **Budget** as the active workbook, select the **View** tab and in the **Window** group click **Hide**. This hides the whole workbook.

3. Click the *Excel* button on the **Taskbar**, check for **Budget** and the **Switch Windows** menu for open workbooks. **Budget** is not displayed in either.

4. Select **Unhide** from the **Window** group.

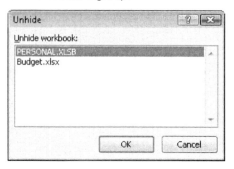

Personal is a workbook that stores global macros, if never used previously it will not be displayed

5. Select **Budget**. Click **OK** to restore it.

6. Make **Spires** active. Click on the **Rates** sheet. This sheet contains the **Tax** and **Vat** rates.

7. Using the **Home** tab, **Cells** group, select **Format** then **Hide & Unhide** then **Hide Sheet**. The **Rates** sheet is no longer visible, although the contents are used in the **Accounts** sheet.

ℹ *Alternatively, right click on a sheet tab and select Hide.*

8. The sheet is hidden until it is restored. Saving the workbook leaves the sheet hidden. Using the **Home** tab, **Cells** group, select **Format** then **Hide & Unhide** and finally **Unhide Sheet**.

9. With the **Rates** sheet selected, click **OK** to restore it.

10. Close all the open workbooks <u>without</u> saving.

Driving Lesson 17 - Revision: Protection

This is not an ECDL test. Testing may only be carried out through certified ECDL test centres. This covers the features introduced in this section. Try not to refer to the preceding Driving Lessons while completing it.

1.   Open the workbook **Easy**. All cells in the worksheet have been **unlocked**.

2.   This worksheet stretches from **A1** to **N14**, but has some data hidden. Unhide the data so that the full worksheet is visible.

3.   Make the following ranges **locked**:

> **B4:M4**
> **B10:M10**
> **B14:M14**
> **N1:N14**

4.   Add the sheet protection without a password.

5.   Enter the **Password to open** as **Pass** and save the workbook as **Protect**.

6.   Close the workbook.

7.   Open the workbook **Protect**.

8.   Remove the workbook password and add the password **007** as a **Password to modify**. Click **Yes** to replace the existing file.

9.   Close the workbook.

10.   Open the workbook **Protect**, enter the password **007** to be able to modify.

11.   Remove the password and save the workbook using the same file name without any password protection. At the prompt to replace the existing file select **Yes**.

12.   Close the workbook.

If you experienced any difficulty completing this Revision refer back to the Driving Lessons in this section. Then redo the Revision.

Once you are confident with the features, complete the Record of Achievement Matrix referring to the section at the end of the guide. Only when competent move on to the next Section.

Section 4

Cell Comments

By the end of this Section you should be able to:

> **Use Cell Comments**
>
> **Display Comments**
>
> **Create, Edit and Delete Comments**

To gain an understanding of the above features, work through the **Driving Lessons** in this **Section**.

For each **Driving Lesson**, read the **Park and Read** instructions, without touching the keyboard, then work through the numbered steps of the **Manoeuvres** on the computer. Complete the **Revision Exercise(s)** at the end of the section to test your knowledge.

Driving Lesson 18 - Cell Comments

🅿 Park and Read

A **Comment** is a piece of text that is attached to a cell. Depending on which options are set, comments are not usually displayed on the worksheet, but a **comment indicator** (a small red triangle) shows where the comments are. They can be easily viewed by moving the mouse pointer over the relevant cell.

Manoeuvres

1.　Open the workbook **Comments**.

2.　Some of the cells on the sheet have red triangles in the corners. These cells have comments attached. Place the mouse pointer on cell **D7**, which has a comment indicator (a small red triangle).

3.　Leave the mouse pointer over the cell for a while and a box will appear containing the comment for that cell.

Division	Sales	Profit	Employees
North	£112,000	Very impressive sales. Pay a bonus.	
South	£97,456		
East	£102,765		
West	£66,833		

ℹ️ *If the comment indicator cannot be seen, click the **File** tab then select **Options** and in the **Advanced** section under **Display** select the required option. The **No comments or indicators** option hides both the comments and indicators, **Comments and indicators** option displays both, select the **Indicators only, and comments on hover** option and click **OK**.*

4.　Place the mouse over the other cells containing comments in turn and view them.

5.　Leave the workbook **Comments** open.

Driving Lesson 19 - Display Comments

▣ Park and Read

Comments can be set to display permanently. The **Review** tab is used to manipulate the comments.

⟨ Manoeuvres

1. The workbook **Comments** should still be open. If not, open it.

2. Display the **Review** tab and in the **Comments** group click the **Show All Comments** button.

3. The **Show All Comments** button displays or hides all the comments. Click the **Show All Comments** button again, all the comments are hidden.

4. To show the **Comments** in turn, the **Next**, or **Previous** buttons are used. Click in cell **A1**. Click the **Next** button. This displays the **Comment** in **D7** in **Edit** mode.

5. Use the **Next** and **Previous** buttons to scroll from comment to comment. An information message is displayed when the end or beginning of the workbook is reached. Click **OK** if this message is displayed.

6. Click on cell **D7** and click the **Show/Hide Comment** button, ⬚ Show/Hide Comment . This displays an individual comment permanently until hidden. (The same button also hides a displayed comment).

7. Right click on cell **D7** and select **Hide Comment** from the shortcut menu.

ℹ️ *Comments can be shown or hidden using the **Review** tab (for multiple comments) or the **Shortcut Menu** from a cell (for a single comment).*

8. Leave the workbook **Comments** open.

Driving Lesson 20 - Create, Edit and Delete Comments

▣ Park and Read

Comments can be inserted anywhere in a spreadsheet and any text can be added. Text in comments can be edited and comments can be deleted.

⌐ Manoeuvres

1.   The workbook **Comments** should still be open. If not, open it.

2.   To create a comment attached to cell **E10**, right click on **E10** and select **Insert Comment** from the shortcut menu.

ⓘ *Alternatively click on the cell and then click the **New Comment** button, on the Review tab.*

3.   In the **Comment** box, the user name is added automatically to the top line of the comment, delete it and type **We must improve this figure**.

4.   Adjust the size of the **Comment Box** (using the handles). Move the box away from the numbers, by placing the cursor on any edge and clicking and dragging (the cursor changes to a four headed arrow when over the box).

5.   Click away from the comment to complete it. The comment indicator is now displayed in the cell **E10**.

6.   Move the mouse over cell **E10** to display the **Comment**. The temporary display is next to the cell.

7.   Move the mouse on to cell **D7** and display that **Comment**. Right click on cell **D7** and select **Edit Comment**.

ⓘ *Alternatively select **Edit Comment** from the **Comments** group.*

8.   Use the <**Backspace**> key to delete the second sentence and edit the comment to **We cannot afford a bonus**. Reduce the size of the comment box and move it away from the numbers.

9.   To remove the note attached to cell **F7**, right click on cell **F7** and select **Delete Comment**. The comment is deleted and the comment indicator is removed.

ⓘ *Alternatively place the cursor in the cell with a comment to delete and click the **Delete** button in the **Comments** group.*

10.   Close the workbook **Comments** <u>without</u> saving.

Driving Lesson 21 - Revision: Cell Comments

This is not an ECDL test. Testing may only be carried out through certified ECDL test centres. This covers the features introduced in this section. Try not to refer to the preceding Driving Lessons while completing it.

1. Open the workbook **Budget**.

2. Add the comment **Why the sudden drop in sales?** to cell **J2**.

3. Add the comment **Consider increasing the price** to cell **B3**.

4. Add the comment **Too many employees?** to cell **B5**.

5. Add the comment **This loss needs to be turned into a profit!** to cell **J14**.

6. Using the **Print** options screen, change the page orientation to **Landscape** and select the option to fit the sheet on one page. Click the **Page Setup** button and on the **Sheet** tab, select **At end of sheet** from the **Comments** area.

7. **Print** a copy of the worksheet and the comments.

i *The comments are printed on a second page.*

8. **Show** all the comments on the worksheet.

9. **Hide** the comment attached to cell **J2**.

10. Edit the comment in cell **J14** to read **This loss at the end of year needs to be turned into a profit.**

11. **Delete** the comment attached to cell **B3**.

12. **Hide** all displayed comments.

13. Close the workbook <u>without</u> saving.

If you experienced any difficulty completing this Revision refer back to the Driving Lessons in this section. Then redo the Revision.

Once you are confident with the features, complete the Record of Achievement Matrix referring to the section at the end of the guide. Only when competent move on to the next Section.

Section 5
Names

By the end of this Section you should be able to:

Use Names

Create and Delete Names for Cell Ranges

Paste and Apply Names

Use Names in Formulas

Use Names with Go To

To gain an understanding of the above features, work through the **Driving Lessons** in this **Section**.

For each **Driving Lesson**, read the **Park and Read** instructions, without touching the keyboard, then work through the numbered steps of the **Manoeuvres** on the computer. Complete the **Revision Exercise(s)** at the end of the section to test your knowledge.

Driving Lesson 22 - Names

ⓟ Park and Read

Names can be used to represent the contents of a cell or a range of cells to make referencing them easier.

For example, a formula might be **=D34-D67**, and the cell references would have to be traced back to see what they represent. If **D34** represents income and **D67** represents expenditure, **Names** could be used so that the same formula can be entered as:

= Income - Expenditure

making it easier for anyone viewing the formula to understand what it is.

Any cell in a worksheet can be given a name by using the **Define Name** command or by typing directly into the **Name Box**. For this name to be used as a reference in formulas, the command **Apply Names** must be used.

Manoeuvres

1. Open the workbook **Vat**.

2. In **C6** enter the formula to calculate the **VAT**. Remember, this will have to use **Absolute Addressing**. The formula is **=C5*$B$15**.

3. Copy this formula across the row into **D6** and **E6**.

4. Complete the **Total Price** row, adding the **Price** to the **VAT**. Do not use **AutoSum**.

5. Click on cell **B15**, the **VAT Rate**. Enter the new rate of **17.5%** (include the % sign).

6. The use of **Names** would make the formulas in this worksheet easier to understand. Click on cell **B15** and from the **Formulas** tab, select **Define Name** from the **Defined Names** group.

continued over

Driving Lesson 22 - Continued

7. The **New Name** dialog box shows any **Names** already defined in the workbook (none in this case) and may suggest a name for the selected cell (**VAT_Rate**). It also displays where the name **Refers to** (Vat!$B$15). The suggested name may be overwritten, but as **VAT_Rate** is a suitable name, click **OK**.

ⓘ *New Name picks its suggestions from any nearby labels but replaces spaces with underscores as spaces are not allowed in **Names**. If there are no suitable suggestions the **Name** box will be blank.*

8. Note that the **Name Box** (above the column **A** heading) now contains the name of the cell, **VAT_Rate**.

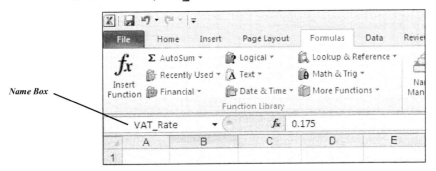

9. Move to cell **C6**. The cell contents still reference **$B$15**. The cell has been named but the name is not used anywhere yet.

10. Select **Apply Names** from the **Define Name** drop down list.

11. A list of available names is displayed, but in this case, just **VAT_Rate**. Click on **OK** to apply this name to the worksheet.

12. Note that the formula in **C6** now shows **C5*VAT_Rate**. The other **VAT** cells are similar.

13. Cells and ranges can also be named by selecting the required cell/s and then typing directly into the **Name Box**. Select the range **C5:E5** and type the name **Price** in the **Name Box** and press **<Enter>** to complete the naming process.

14. Click away from the range and click the **Name Box** drop down and select **VAT_Rate**, cell **B15** is highlighted. Display the **Price** range, the named range **C5:E5** is highlighted.

ⓘ *Single cells can be named and used in exactly the same way.*

15. Save the workbook as **Vat2**.

16. Leave the workbook open for the next Driving Lesson.

Driving Lesson 23 - Using Names in Formulas

🅿 Park and Read

As well as manually defining **Names** for individual cells, they can be automatically created for ranges of cells based on existing row and column headers, using the **Create from Selection** button.

Existing **Names** can be used in new formulas by typing the cell name or by using the **Use in Formula** drop down **Paste** command.

Manoeuvres

1. Open the workbook **Vat2** if it is not already open.

2. Select the range **B4:E7**.

3. Click the **Create from Selection** button in the **Defined Names** group on the **Formulas** tab.

4. Make sure **Top row** and **Left column** are selected. Click **OK** to create names based on the row and column headers for the selected range.

5. Select **Apply Names** from the **Define Name** drop down to display all the names just created. The new names should be highlighted. Click **OK** to apply these names to all formulas.

6. Select **C7** to see names used in the formula rather than cell references. Look at other cells containing formulas.

7. Insert a column between **March** and **Total**. In **F4** enter **April** and in **F5** type **5050**.

8. In **F6** type **=F5*** and then click **Use in Formula**.

9. Select **VAT_Rate** from the displayed list. The name is pasted into the formula. Press <**Enter**> to complete the formula.

10. Enter the appropriate formula in **F7** to add the **Total Price** for April. Note that as **Column F** was added after creating the names it is not included in the named ranges.

ℹ️ *To include names in the new column, the names have to be redefined. It is better to leave the creating and applying of names until after the spreadsheet structure has been completed.*

11. Check the formulas in the **Total** column to make sure that they include the new figures.

12. Save the workbook **Vat2** and leave it open for the next Driving Lesson.

Driving Lesson 24 - Using Go To with Names

🅿 Park and Read

The **Go To** command can not only be used to move quickly to a cell by typing its reference, but also to move to any named cell or range.

🗝 Manoeuvres

1.   Open the workbook **Vat2** if it is not already open.

2.   Display the **Home** tab and from the **Editing** group, select **Go To** from the **Find & Select** drop down.

ℹ️ *Alternatively the key press <**Ctrl G**> or the function key <**F5**> can be used.*

3.   All the names on the sheet are listed. Click **VAT_Rate** and then **OK**.

4.   The cell containing the **VAT_Rate**, i.e. **B15**, is now the active cell.

5.   Press <**F5**>, the **Go To** key. Select **January** from the list and click **OK**. The range of cells named **January** is highlighted.

6.   Close the workbook <u>without</u> saving.

7.   Open the workbook **Accounts**.

8.   Press <**F5**>, the **Go To** key. There is a long list of all the named ranges in this sheet. Select **Materials** then **OK**. The range containing the **Materials** figures will be highlighted. Use the horizontal scroll bar to view the whole range if necessary.

9.   Select **Go To** from the **Find & Select** drop down, choose **Budget** and click **OK**. The figures for the whole spreadsheet are now highlighted.

10.   This named range is now not required, to delete it select **Name Manager** in the **Defined Names** group on the **Formulas** tab.

11.   Click on **Budget** in the list and then click the **Delete** button.

12.   Click **OK** to complete the removal of the range name.

13.   Close the **Name Manager** dialog box.

14.   Press <**F5**>, the **Go To** key and check the list for **Budget**. The name has been deleted. Click **Cancel**.

15.   Close the workbook <u>without</u> saving.

Driving Lesson 25 - Revision: Names

This is not an ECDL test. Testing may only be carried out through certified ECDL test centres. This covers the features introduced in this section. Try not to refer to the preceding Driving Lessons while completing it.

1.   Open the workbook **Cashflow**.

2.   Create names for the whole worksheet, i.e. **A3:N29**.

3.   Apply the names just created, except for **Payments**.

4.   Examine the formulas, especially for **Turnover**, **Spending** and **Gross Profit**.

5.   What is now the formula for **February's Spending**?

6.   Move to cell **A32** and type **=Bar September** to find the amount income from the **Bar** sales in **September**.

7.   Freeze the panes with the active cell as **B4**.

8.   Check the **Bar** receipts for **September** using the main worksheet content. Do they match?

9.   Similarly, in **A34** display the income from hiring out **Function Rooms** in **December** (you will need to use an underscore symbol in labels consisting of 2 or more words).

10. What formula did you use?

11. **Go To** the **Gross Profit** figures and make them bold.

12. All the **Gross Profit** cells display the same formula. In **A36** display the **Gross Profit** for **July** using **Names** in a formula.

13. **Go To** the **Receipts** and format all the values with no decimal places.

14. Save the workbook as **Cashflow2**.

15. Close the workbook.

---

[i]   *Answers are shown in the **Answers** section at the end of the guide.*

If you experienced any difficulty completing this Revision refer back to the Driving Lessons in this section. Then redo the Revision.

Once you are confident with the features, complete the Record of Achievement Matrix referring to the section at the end of the guide. Only when competent move on to the next Section.

Section 6
Templates

By the end of this Section you should be able to:

Create and Understand Templates

Use Templates

Edit Templates

To gain an understanding of the above features, work through the **Driving Lessons** in this **Section**.

For each **Driving Lesson**, read the **Park and Read** instructions, without touching the keyboard, then work through the numbered steps of the **Manoeuvres** on the computer. Complete the **Revision Exercise(s)** at the end of the section to test your knowledge.

Driving Lesson 26 - Creating a Template

🅿 Park and Read

A **Template** is a base worksheet that has been prepared ready for data to be entered. It can contain: text, graphics, formulas, protection, macros and formatting. Using a template ensures consistency of appearance and performance for the spreadsheets based on it.

Templates are created by specifying a **Save as type** of **Template** when saving. They are given a file extension of **.xltx** which distinguishes them from normal workbooks.

⌇ Manoeuvres

1. Open the workbook **Budget**. This represents the budget data for a small company.

2. To change this workbook into a template, the base data must be removed, leaving the formulas. Delete the data in the ranges **B2:M3**, **B5:M6** and **B8:M9**.

3. To save this workbook as a **Template**, click the **File** tab and select **Save As** from the menu.

4. In **Save as type**, choose **Excel Template**.

5. Notice how the location for the saved file changes automatically to the **Templates** folder. Click **Save**. The workbook is then saved as a template and stored with other templates in the **Templates** folder.

6. Close the **Budget** template.

Driving Lesson 27 - Using a Template

🅿 Park and Read

A template can be opened repeatedly and used as the base for many other spreadsheets. These are saved as workbooks with new names to leave the original template unaffected.

Manoeuvres

1. To use a template, click the **File** tab and then **New**.

2. Click the **My templates** icon to display the **New** dialog box showing the **Personal Templates** tab.

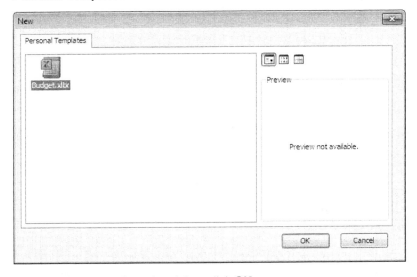

3. Ensure **Budget** is selected and then click **OK**.

4. The **template** is opened and the name changed. Data can now be added. Add some data to column **B** to see if the formulas work.

5. The name is similar in use to the default workbook names **Book1**, etc. To save the template as a workbook, click the **File** tab and select either **Save** or **Save As** to display the **Save As** dialog box.

6. Save the workbook as **Budget2** (take care to save to the required location; **AM4 Excel 2010 Data**, not the **Templates** folder and make sure that the **Save as type** is **Excel Workbook**).

7. Start a new workbook based on the **Budget** template. Compare the open workbooks by making each one active in turn.

8. Close both the workbooks <u>without</u> saving.

Driving Lesson 28 - Editing a Template

▣ Park and Read

If required, templates can be resaved as templates with the same file name, allowing the original template to be overwritten to incorporate changes.

↱ Manoeuvres

1. Start a **New** workbook based on the **Budget** template.

2. Change all the tax rates to **40%**.

3. Change the orientation of the page to landscape and ensure that the spreadsheet fits onto one page.

4. Format the numbers within rows **2 to 4**, **6 to 11**, **13 & 14** as currency with 2 decimal places.

5. To resave the template, click the **File** tab and then select **Save As**.

6. Change the **Save as type** to **Excel Template (*.xltx)** and enter the file name **Budget**.

7. Click **Save**.

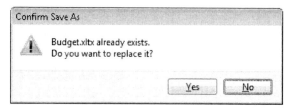

8. A dialog box appears informing that the **Budget** file already exists, click **Yes** to overwrite the original template. Close the **Budget** template.

9. Open a new workbook based on the template to check that the changes have been made.

10. Close all open workbooks.

11. The created **template** is to be deleted. Click the **File** tab then **New**.

12. Click the **My templates** option, the **New** dialog box is displayed. The templates are displayed with 🗒 icons (a yellow stripe along the top of a pad of pages). Right click on **Budget** and from the shortcut menu select **Delete**. Click **Yes** to confirm the deletion and **Cancel** the dialog box.

13. Click **My templates** to display the **New** dialog box to check that the template has been successfully deleted.

14. Click **Cancel** to close the **New** dialog box.

Driving Lesson 29 - Revision: Templates

This is not an ECDL test. Testing may only be carried out through certified ECDL test centres. This covers the features introduced in this section. Try not to refer to the preceding Driving Lessons while completing it.

1.   Open the workbook **Retail** and delete all the values on rows **2**, **3** and **5** to **9**, be careful not to delete the formulas in column **N**.

2.   Save the workbook as a **Template**, using the same name and close it.

3.   Open a new workbook based on the **Retail** template.

4.   To add data to the template, open the workbook **Retail Data**.

5.   Copy and paste the data in range **A3:L4** from **Retail Data** to **B2** in **Retail1** and the range **A6:L10** to **B5**.

6.   Save the workbook in the data folder as **Retail2**.

7.   Close the workbook. Close **Retail Data**.

8.   The **Retail** template is to be deleted. Display the **templates** on your computer.

9.   Right click on the **Retail** template and select **Delete**.

10.   Click **Yes** to confirm the deletion.

11.   Check that the template **Retail** has been deleted.

12.   Cancel any open dialog boxes.

If you experienced any difficulty completing this Revision refer back to the Driving Lessons in this section. Then redo the Revision.

Once you are confident with the features, complete the Record of Achievement Matrix referring to the section at the end of the guide. Only when competent move on to the next Section.

Section 7
Formulas

By the end of this Section you should be able to:

Display and Check Formulas

Understand Formulas that Produce Errors

Use Mixed Cell Referencing

Create Custom Number Formats

To gain an understanding of the above features, work through the **Driving Lessons** in this **Section**.

For each **Driving Lesson**, read the **Park and Read** instructions, without touching the keyboard, then work through the numbered steps of the **Manoeuvres** on the computer. Complete the **Revision Exercise(s)** at the end of the section to test your knowledge.

Driving Lesson 30 - Display Formulas

P Park and Read

It is sometimes useful to identify quickly which cells within a worksheet are formulas rather than entered values, and to display the actual formulas on the screen instead of the results. This is particularly relevant when checking whether all formulas are correct. Individual formulas can also be displayed in a way that aids checking.

Manoeuvres

1. Open the workbook **Balance**.

2. To determine which cells in the worksheet are formulas, display the **Home** tab and from the **Editing** group, select **Find & Select** then **Go To Special**.

3. Select **Formulas** and click **OK**. All formula cells are highlighted, showing for example that the numbers in the **Charities** row are not simply entered values but the results of calculations.

4. To show all the formulas on a worksheet, display the **Formulas** tab and click the **Show Formulas** button, 🔲 Show Formulas in the **Formula Auditing** group. All formulas will be shown in full, the columns being widened where necessary.

i   *Alternatively, the key press combination <Ctrl `> can also be used to show or hide the formulas. Press the **Ctrl** and the key under the **Esc** key.*

5. Click the **Show Formulas** again to revert to the normal view (results rather than formulas).

6. Ensure that the worksheet is in normal view and double click on cell **D16**. The formula is displayed in the cell itself with colour coding to show which cells or ranges are used in the formula. So the reference to **C16** is in blue and the cell **C16** is outlined in blue.

7. The worksheet is in **In-cell edit** mode now so that the formula can be amended, by dragging the coloured outlines to different cells or by dragging the **Fill Handle** to extend the range. After checking, press <Enter> (to accept any changes) or <Esc> (to reject any changes) to finish the editing.

8. Leave the workbook **Balance** open.

Driving Lesson 31 - Formulas that Produce Errors

▣ Park and Read

There can be problems when some formulas are calculated, usually because the referenced cells are not as expected. When a formula cannot be calculated the cell displays an error message. Functions **ISERROR** and **ERROR.TYPE** can be used to check for and identify errors.

The following error values (with their error type number) can be found:

#NULL!	1	The two areas specified do not intersect
#DIV/0!	2	Division by zero
#VALUE!	3	The wrong argument used
#REF!	4	Cell referenced is not valid
#NAME?	5	Does not recognise text in a formula
#NUM!	6	Error with number in formula
#N/A	7	The value used in the formula is not available
######		The result is too long to fit into the cell

⌒ Manoeuvres

1.   The workbook **Balance** should still be open. If not, open it.

2.   In cell **H20** enter the function **=ISERROR(H18)** to check whether the formula in **H18** is producing an error. It should read **FALSE**.

3.   In cell **H4**, enter the number **0**. Cell **H18** is now a **#DIV/0!** error because it is trying to divide by **H4**. **H20** should read **TRUE**.

4.   Cell **H18** is displayed with a green triangle. Click on cell **H18**, a **Smart Tag** is displayed, ⬨.

5.   Click on the tag to display a list of options.

6.   The error is shown as a **Divide by Zero Error**. Investigate the available options.

7.   Using the function **IF** can replace errors with a specific value. In cell **H18** enter the formula **=IF(H4=0,0,H16/H4)**. If **H4** is zero the formula is not calculated (so no error and **H20 = FALSE** again) and the value of **0** is returned.

8.   In cell **H4**, enter the character **X**. Cells **H16** and **H18** are now **#VALUE!** errors because both expect cell **H4** to be a numeric value.

9.   In cell **I20** enter the function **=ERROR.TYPE(H18)** to identify any error in cell **H18**. The result is error type **3**.

10.   Close the workbook <u>without</u> saving.

Driving Lesson 32 - Mixed Referencing

🅿 Park and Read

Mixed Referencing is a cross between **Absolute** and **Relative**. One part of the reference is fixed with a **$** symbol and the other part is not, e.g. **$A15** (column **A** fixed) or **A$15** (row **15** fixed).

🖐 Manoeuvres

1. Start a new workbook.

2. Create the following spreadsheet.

	A	B	C	D	E	F	G
1							
2		10%	20%	30%	40%	50%	
3	5						
4	10						
5	15						
6	20						
7	25						
8							

3. In cell **B3** enter the formula **=A3*B2**, to calculate **10%** of **5**.

4. Use the **Fill Handle** to drag the formula across to **F3**.

5. With the range still highlighted, drag the **Fill Handle** down to row **7** to fill the rest of the range.

	A	B	C	D	E	F	G
1							
2		10%	20%	30%	40%	50%	
3	5	0.5	0.1	0.03	0.012	0.006	
4	10	5	0.5	0.015	0.00018	1.08E-06	
5	15	75	37.5	0.5625	0.000101	1.09E-10	
6	20	1500	56250	31640.63	3.203613	3.5E-10	
7	25	37500	2.11E+09	6.67E+13	2.14E+14	74902.76	
8							
9							

6. The result is obviously not what was intended. Double click on cell **D5** to check the formula and which cells it uses. The formula is **=C5*D4** because of **Relative Addressing**.

7. The formula should be **=A5*D2**. Highlight and delete the range **B3:F7**.

8. Try and use **Absolute Referencing** to overcome this problem. In cell **B3** type the formula **=$A$3*$B$2**.

continued over

Driving Lesson 32 - Continued

9.   Drag this formula across to column **F** and then down to row **7**.

10. Double click on cell **D5** to check the formulas and which cells it uses. The formula is **=$A$3*$B$2**, so all of the formulas are now the same, which is still not correct.

	A	B	C	D	E	F	G
1							
2		10%	20%	30%	40%	50%	
3	5	0.5	0.5	0.5	0.5	0.5	
4	10	0.5	0.5	0.5	0.5	0.5	
5	15	0.5	0.5	=$A$3*$B$2		0.5	
6	20	0.5	0.5	0.5	0.5	0.5	
7	25	0.5	0.5	0.5	0.5	0.5	
8							

11. **Mixed Referencing** can be used to fix the column as **A** and row as **2**, allowing the other reference to change, to calculate the formulas.

12. Highlight, then delete the range **B3:F7** again and move back to cell **B3**.

13. Type the formula **=$A3*B$2**, this fixes column **A** and row **2** because the **dollar** signs are before these values in the formula.

14. Drag this new formula across to **F3** and then down to row **7**.

	A	B	C	D	E	F	G
1							
2		10%	20%	30%	40%	50%	
3	5	0.5	1	1.5	2	2.5	
4	10	1	2	3	4	5	
5	15	1.5	3	4.5	6	7.5	
6	20	2	4	6	8	10	
7	25	2.5	5	7.5	10	12.5	
8							
9							

15. Double click in cell **D5** and check that the formula is **=$A5*D$2**.

	A	B	C	D	E	F	G
1							
2		10%	20%	30%	40%	50%	
3	5	0.5	1	1.5	2	2.5	
4	10	1	2	3	4	5	
5	15	1.5	3	=$A5*D$2	6	7.5	
6	20	2	4	6	8	10	
7	25	2.5	5	7.5	10	12.5	
8							

16. Save the workbook as **Mixed**.

17. Close the workbook.

Driving Lesson 33 - Custom Number Formats

🅿 Park and Read

As well as formatting cells using the standard number categories such as **Currency** and **Date**, it is possible to create **Custom** formats using a variety of codes. Some of the available codes are listed below:

d	day number without leading zero, e.g. 5
dd	day number with leading zero, e.g. 05
ddd	day abbreviated as text, e.g. Mon
dddd	day as text, e.g. Monday
m	month without leading zero, e.g. 6 (if used after hh *Excel* assumes minutes)
mm	month with leading zero, e.g. 06
mmm	month abbreviated as text, e.g. Jun
mmmm	month as text, e.g. September
h	hours without leading zero based on 24 hour clock unless used with am/pm
hh	hours with leading zero based on 24 hour clock unless used with am/pm
[colour]	displays whatever is following in the stated colour Black, Cyan, Magenta, Blue, White, Green, Red and Yellow.
[condition value]	where condition may be <, >, =, >=, <=, <> and value can be any number
#	displays only significant digits
0	displays leading zeros, e.g. 023, one number is represented by one zero, i.e. 000. Letters can also be used with zeros to add a prefix or a suffix to a custom number, e.g. K000 or 000G to display K023 and 023G.
?	adds spaces either side of decimal point
,	thousands separator
.	decimal separator

🐾 Manoeuvres

1. Start a new workbook. In cell **B2** enter **56**. Click back on cell **B2** and with the **Home** tab selected, click **Format** then select **Format Cells**, to display the **Format Cells** dialog box.

2. In the **Number** tab, normal formatting is achieved by using the standard categories of **General**, **Number**, **Currency**, **Percentage**, etc. Click **Custom** to display the list from which to select and optionally amend.

continued over

Driving Lesson 33 - Continued

3.   The **Type** box is where the custom format is created. Scroll down the list of built-in **Types**. Select one and check how it affects the display in the **Sample** box.

4.   Select the second item in the list **0**, edit this in the **Type** box to display 4 numbers followed by **K**, i.e. **0000K**. The sample shows **0056K** (very useful when creating components or part numbers that contain letters with the numbers). Click **OK**.

 The built-in format used as a starting point for a custom format is still unchanged and available to use.

5.   In cell **B4** press **<Ctrl ;>** to enter today's date, press **<Enter>**. Click on cell **B4**, display the **Format Cells** dialog box and click the **Custom** category.

6.   To create a custom date, select a date format to work from, choose **dd-mmm-yy**. Edit this in the **Type** box to read **ddd dd mmmm yy**.

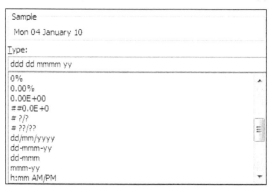

7.   Check the **Sample** box and click **OK**. Column **B** is widened to display the date.

8.   Enter your birth date in cell **B6** in the form **dd/mm/yyyy**.

9.   **Format** this date using the **Custom** date format already created, the **Custom Formats** are stored at the end of the list. This displays the day as well as the date on which you were born.

10. Close the workbook <u>without</u> saving.

Driving Lesson 34 - Revision: Formulas

This is not an ECDL test. Testing may only be carried out through certified ECDL test centres. This covers the features introduced in this section. Try not to refer to the preceding Driving Lessons while completing it.

1. Open the workbook **Errors**. This workbook contains a variety of faults, some of which are incorrect ranges in functions that are not shown as errors.

2. Correct any errors that are contained in any of the formulas. For the division by zero error, replace the formulas in that column with an **IF** statement that replaces the error with zero when it occurs.

3. Format the range **J4:K10** with a custom number format to display percentages with one decimal place.

4. In the range **C3:G3** enter the actual dates for last week. Format the range **C3:G3** with custom dates to display a **2** digit day, followed by a - then a two digit month, e.g. 03-05 for May 3rd.

5. The range **A4:A9** contains employee numbers. Some contain 3 digits, some 4 and some 5. Use a custom number format on the range so that all the numbers are **6** digits (use the format **000000**) to add the leading zeros.

6. Check cell **K10**, it should be **100.0%** if the formulas are correct.

7. Print a copy of the worksheet.

8. Close the workbook <u>without</u> saving.

ℹ️ *Answers are shown in the **Answers** section at the end of the guide.*

If you experienced any difficulty completing this Revision refer back to the Driving Lessons in this section. Then redo the Revision.

Once you are confident with the features, complete the Record of Achievement Matrix referring to the section at the end of the guide. Only when competent move on to the next Section.

Section 8
Outlines

By the end of this Section you should be able to:

Create an Outline

Expand and Collapse Outline Level Details

To gain an understanding of the above features, work through the **Driving Lessons** in this **Section**.

For each **Driving Lesson**, read the **Park and Read** instructions, without touching the keyboard, then work through the numbered steps of the **Manoeuvres** on the computer. Complete the **Revision Exercise(s)** at the end of the section to test your knowledge.

Driving Lesson 35 - Creating an Outline

🅿 Park and Read

An **Outline** is used to hide parts of a worksheet, making it easier to see the more important areas. Different users may need to see different information or different amounts of information.

An outline can show up to eight different **levels**, both horizontally and vertically, with each level showing a different amount of data. The levels are **displayed** or **hidden** to show the required data.

👆 Manoeuvres

1. Open the workbook **House**.

2. Display the **Data** tab, click the **Group** button drop down and select **Auto Outline**.

ℹ️   *Excel assumes that the summary rows (the formulas) are at the bottom of the detail and the summary columns are to the right.*

*Level
Buttons*

*Row
Level
Bars*

*Hide
Buttons*

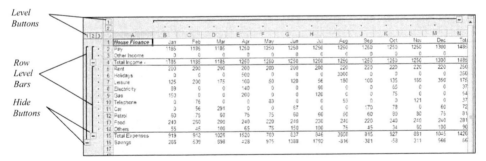

3. The outline has been created. It has 3 row levels and 2 column levels. Notice the various buttons and bars above and to the left of the worksheet.

4. The **Hide** detail symbol ⊟, hides rows or columns in an outline level when clicked. Click the **Hide** button next to row **15** to hide rows 5 to 14.

5. The **Show** detail symbol ⊞, indicates hidden rows or columns. Click on the button, ⊞, next to row **15** to expand the hidden rows.

continued over

Driving Lesson 35 - Continued

6.   Row and column level buttons, [1][2][3], indicate the number of levels in an outline. Click on them to display a specific level - the lower the number, the less detail is displayed. Click on row level **1** and column level **1**.

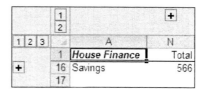

7.   Click on the row level **3** button and the column level **2** button to fully expand the **Outline**.

8.   The row and column level bars indicate the range of data in a level. Click on them to hide the data, as an alternative to using the **Hide** detail button. Click on the detail level bar across the columns to hide the columns **B** to **M**.

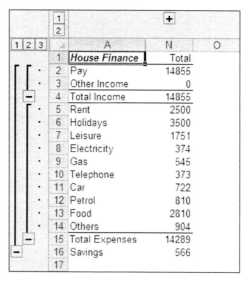

9.   Expand the columns to full view using any method.

10. To remove the **Auto Outline**, click the **Ungroup** drop down and select **Clear Outline**. The outline is removed.

11. Close the workbook <u>without</u> saving.

Driving Lesson 36 - Working with an Outline

▣ Park and Read

Outlines are used to restrict the amount of data seen on a worksheet. When an outline is created, the levels appear around summary rows and columns, as these are usually the most important areas of a worksheet. Levels can be expanded and collapsed using the buttons described in the last exercise.

⌒ Manoeuvres

1.   Open the workbook **Retail**.

2.   Add an **Auto Outline** to the worksheet by clicking the **Group** button drop down from the **Data** tab and selecting **Auto Outline**.

3.   The outline is fully expanded. It has 4 row levels and 2 column levels. Hide the first row level by clicking on the row level button **3**. This is one level down.

4.   Hide the rows by clicking on the **Hide Detail** symbol, ⊟, for the **first** level. The worksheet now only shows three rows.

5.   Hide the columns by clicking on the column level button **1**. The worksheet is now fully collapsed, showing only **Tax** and **Net Profit**, rows **1**, **13** and **14**.

6.   Display the rows to the **third** level by clicking on the row level button **3**.

7.   Click on the **Hide detail** symbol next to row **11** to hide the **Turnover** and **Spending** rows.

8.   Practise showing and hiding levels using the ⊞ and ⊟ symbols.

9.   To remove the **Auto Outline**, click the **Ungroup** button drop down and select **Clear Outline**. The outline is removed.

10.   Rows and columns can be highlighted and an outline added manually if the **Auto Outline** is not satisfactory. Select rows **2** and **3**, using the row headings (numbers) then click the **Group** button to add an outline level to row **4**.

11.   Highlight rows **5** to **9** and group them to add an outline.

12.   Highlight rows **2** to **13** and group them to add another outline level.

continued over

Driving Lesson 36 - Continued

13. Highlight columns **B** to **M** and group them to add a horizontal outline. An **Outline** has now been manually created with 3 row levels and 2 column levels, as shown below:

	A	B	C	D	E	F	G	H	I	J	K	L	M	N
1	Retail	Jan	Feb	Mar	Apr	May	Jun	Jul	Aug	Sep	Oct	Nov	Dec	Total
2	Sales	2600	2000	2200	2700	3000	3200	2500	1500	1600	2500	6800	8000	38600
3	Article	8.99	8.99	8.99	8.99	8.99	8.99	8.99	8.99	8.99	8.99	8.99	8.99	8.99
4	Turnover	23374	17980	19778	24273	26970	28768	22475	13485	14384	22475	61132	71920	347014
5	Stock	4000	3000	6000	8000	8000	7000	3000	4000	10000	12000	15000	14000	94000
6	Promotion	0	0	2500	0	0	2000	0	0	2000	8000	8000	4000	26500
7	Advertising	320	350	450	320	450	350	320	400	300	280	1000	1200	5740
8	Wages	2400	2400	2400	2400	2400	2400	2400	2400	2400	2400	3200	3200	30400
9	Overheads	2800	2500	2000	2000	2000	2000	2000	2000	2000	3000	3500	4000	29800
10	Spending	9520	8250	13350	12720	12850	13750	7720	8800	16700	25680	30700	26400	186440
11	Profit	13854	9730	6428	11553	14120	15018	14755	4685	-2316	-3205	30432	45520	160574
12	Tax rate	50%	50%	50%	50%	50%	50%	50%	50%	50%	50%	50%	50%	50%
13	Tax	6927	4865	3214	5777	7060	7509	7378	2343	0	0	15216	22760	83048
14	Net Profit	6927	4865	3214	5777	7060	7509	7378	2343	-2316	-3205	15216	22760	77527
15														

14. Collapse all the levels.

15. Expand all the levels and highlight rows **2** and **3**, then click the **Ungroup** button to remove a part of the **Outline**.

16. To remove the whole outline, click on any cell and then click the **Ungroup** button drop down and select **Clear Outline** as before. The outline is removed.

17. Close the workbook <u>without</u> saving.

Driving Lesson 37 - Revision: Outlines

This is not an ECDL test. Testing may only be carried out through certified ECDL test centres. This covers the features introduced in this section. Try not to refer to the preceding Driving Lessons while completing it.

1.   Open the workbook **Spires**.

2.   View a preview of the worksheet.

3.   Add an **Auto Outline** to the worksheet.

4.   Display the row level **3**.

5.   Set the display to **Landscape** and fit to one page.

6.   Obtain a printed copy.

7.   Remove the **Auto Outline**.

8.   Create a manual outline by grouping rows **4** to **13** and rows **18** to **29**.

9.   Collapse the rows.

10. Print a copy of the outlined worksheet.

11. Remove the **Outline** on rows **4** to **13**.

12. Close the workbook <u>without</u> saving.

If you experienced any difficulty completing this Revision refer back to the Driving Lessons in this section. Then redo the Revision.

Once you are confident with the features, complete the Record of Achievement Matrix referring to the section at the end of the guide. Only when competent move on to the next Section.

Section 9
Scenarios

By the end of this Section you should be able to:

Create Scenarios

Use, Edit and Delete Scenarios

Create Scenario Summary Reports

To gain an understanding of the above features, work through the **Driving Lessons** in this **Section**.

For each **Driving Lesson**, read the **Park and Read** instructions, without touching the keyboard, then work through the numbered steps of the **Manoeuvres** on the computer. Complete the **Revision Exercise(s)** at the end of the section to test your knowledge.

Driving Lesson 38 - Creating Scenarios

P Park and Read

When a worksheet is used as a model, certain key input values are varied to see the effect on the resulting solutions. Separate versions of the worksheet, showing different input values and solutions, can be saved as **Scenarios**. This helps in "What-If?" situations, where various solutions can be named and be displayed to compare, for example, the best and worst cases.

Manoeuvres

1. Open the workbook **Food**, which shows the ingredients available to make 3 products and the profit from each product. Varying the production mix for each product (**F5:H5**) will produce different total profit. For the first model ensure that the cells **F5:H5** are all **0**.

2. Highlight the range **F5:H5**. Display the **Data** tab, and from the **Data Tools** group, click [What-If Analysis ▾]. Select **Scenario Manager**.

3. In the **Scenario Manager** dialog box, click **Add** and enter the **Scenario name** as **Worst**. Make sure the **Changing cells** are F5:H5, then click **OK**.

4. Leave the values of the three changing cells as **0** and click **OK**. **Worst** is now displayed in the **Scenario** list.

5. The next scenario will be a guess to try and maximise the profit. Click **Add**, enter the name as **Guess** and click **OK**. Enter the values of the 3 cells as **100, 120** and **110**.

6. Click **OK**. Click **Show** to see the results with these values.

7. The next scenario will be another guess to try and maximise the profit. Click **Add**, enter the name as **Guess2** and click **OK**. Enter the values of the 3 cells as **150, 150** and **160**. Click **OK**.

8. Click **Add** again, enter the name as **Best** and click **OK**. This **Scenario** will use figures that have been calculated elsewhere (using **Solver** - not included in this syllabus) to produce the best possible value of **Profit**, **G17**. Enter the values of the 3 cells as **159, 167** and **200**, and click **OK**.

9. Click **Close**. Four scenarios have now been created. Save the workbook as **Scenario** and leave it open.

Driving Lesson 39 - Using, Editing and Deleting Scenarios

▣ Park and Read

Once a set of **Scenarios** have been created, they can be viewed by selecting the required scenario from the list. **Scenarios** can also be edited and deleted using the **Scenario Manager** dialog box.

↱ Manoeuvres

1.   The workbook **Scenario** should still be open. If not, open it.

2.   Display the **Scenario Manager** from the **What-If Analysis** drop down. The four created scenarios are displayed in the list.

3.   The scenario **Guess2** is not wanted, to delete it, click on **Guess2** and then click **Delete**. The **Guess2** scenario is removed from the list.

4.   Select **Best** then select **Show** (the dialog box may have to be moved to see the values on the worksheet). The values and the solution for the **Best** scenario are now displayed. Note that most of the ingredients are used. Make a mental note of the **Total Profit**.

5.   Show the **Guess** scenario. Note the **Total Profit** now.

6.   Show the **Worst** scenario, click **Edit** and **OK**. The worst scenario can now be changed. Change the values so that they are all **50**. Click on **OK**.

7.   Click **Show** to view the results then close the **Scenario Manager** dialog box.

8.   Save the workbook using the same name and leave it open.

Driving Lesson 40 - Scenario Summary Report

🅿 Park and Read

A **Scenario Summary Report** is a report that lists all the scenarios created for a worksheet, along with the **result cells**.

🖐 Manoeuvres

1. The workbook **Scenario** should still be open. If not, open it.

2. Display the **Scenario Manager**. Click on **Summary**.

3. The **Result cell** is the **Total Profit**, **G17**. Click on the cell **G17**. Move the dialog box if necessary.

4. Click **OK**. The **Summary Report** is now displayed.

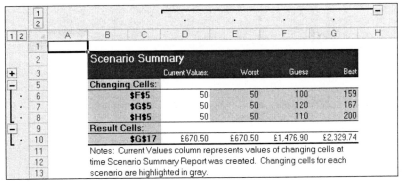

5. The report shows the values of the changing cells and the result cell for each scenario. An **outline view**, is provided, allowing certain rows and columns to be grouped or un-grouped. The outline can be manipulated to change the view of the data. The details of this process are covered in the **Adding Sub Totals** Driving Lesson.

6. Note that the report is created on a separate sheet called **Scenario Summary** within the current workbook.

7. Save the workbook using the same name and then close it.

Driving Lesson 41 - Revision: Scenarios

This is not an ECDL test. Testing may only be carried out through certified ECDL test centres. This covers the features introduced in this section. Try not to refer to the preceding Driving Lessons while completing it.

1.   Open the workbook **Mailshot**.

2.   The range **C7:C9** should be empty, if not delete the contents of the range.

3.   Display the **Scenario Manager** and add the scenario: **Guess1** with the values for **C7:C9** as **800, 700** and **500**.

4.   Add the scenario: **Guess2** with the values for **C7:C9** as **1000, 600** and **400**.

5.   Add the scenario: **Guess3** with the values for **C7:C9** as **750, 750** and **500**.

6.   The three **Scenarios** are now named. Display **Guess2**.

7.   Change the orientation to **Landscape** and print a copy of the worksheet.

8.   Use the **Scenario Manager** to produce a **Scenario Summary**, the **Result Cell** is **I11**.

9.   Print a copy of the **Scenario Summary**.

10.   Display **Sheet1** and use the **Scenario Manager** to delete the Scenario **Guess3**.

11.   Save the workbook as **Mailshot Scenarios**.

12.   Close the workbook.

If you experienced any difficulty completing this Revision refer back to the Driving Lessons in this section. Then redo the Revision.

Once you are confident with the features, complete the Record of Achievement Matrix referring to the section at the end of the guide. Only when competent move on to the next Section.

Section 10
Linking & Importing

By the end of this Section you should be able to:

Link Cells

Link between Worksheets and Workbooks

Link to a Word Document

Use Hyperlinks

Importing Delimited Data

Consolidate using 3D-Sum

To gain an understanding of the above features, work through the **Driving Lessons** in this **Section**.

For each **Driving Lesson**, read the **Park and Read** instructions, without touching the keyboard, then work through the numbered steps of the **Manoeuvres** on the computer. Complete the **Revision Exercise(s)** at the end of the section to test your knowledge.

Driving Lesson 42 - Linking

🅿 Park and Read

A link is a formula reference to a cell in the same sheet, another sheet in the same workbook or to another workbook. The sheet that contains the link is called the **container** workbook. The workbook pointed to by the link, which has the original data, is known as the **source** workbook. The reference is **live**, which means that if all sheets are open, any changes in the source workbook are automatically seen in the container workbook.

Links can be used to consolidate several related worksheets/workbooks into one. For example, financial information can be collected in separate worksheets from the various divisions within a company, and then gathered together into one workbook to show the overall company results.

Linking data has a number of advantages:

- To share or consolidate information

- To simplify a complex problem by breaking it down into several separate workbooks

- To divide work among several people

- To build models normally too large for memory

- To add flexibility to workbooks

🅿 Manoeuvres

1. Open the workbook **Link Demo** and display the **Consol** sheet. This represents the consolidated results for a company with 3 regions.

2. Click on **C8**. The formula contains a reference to cell **C7** so that if **C7** changes, so will **C8**. This is the simplest form of link.

3. The range **C6** to **F7** contains references like **South!C6**. This is a link referring to the cell **C6** on sheet named **South**.

4. Note the profit figure for the **Fourth Quarter** (**-£1282**, i.e. a loss) then switch to the worksheet **South**.

5. Change the value in cell **F6** to **180** and return to the sheet **Consol**. The profit for **Fourth Quarter** has been updated. The profit figure should now be **£7,077**.

ℹ️ *Links can also be made to cells in different workbooks as described in the* ***Linking Between Workbooks*** *Driving Lesson.*

6. Close the workbook <u>without</u> saving.

Driving Lesson 43 - Creating Links

▣ Park and Read

Links to cells on the same worksheet, as in a formula for example, use the simple cell reference, e.g. **=B3+B4**.

Links created between worksheets differ from cell links in that the reference includes the sheet name followed by a **!** e.g. **=Sheet2!C10**.

To create a **Link** within a workbook, copy and paste from one sheet to another or start entering a formula and point to the required cell/s in other sheets.

Charts are either embedded on the data sheet or placed on a new sheet during the creation process. Charts are linked automatically to the base data.

A 3D-sum function can be used to consolidate data from several worksheets. This is like the normal **Sum** function but instead of adding up a column or along a row, it adds corresponding cells across adjacent worksheets.

↱ Manoeuvres

1. Open the workbook **Links**. This shows sales data from 3 regions on separate sheets and a **Results** sheet on which to consolidate the data. Embedded charts have been created from the data on each of the sheets **North**, **South** and **Mid**. The sales and costs figures for the northern region have been charted on a separate sheet named **Chart**.

2. Click on the **North** worksheet. Charts are linked to the data automatically. Click on cell **D6** and type **5000** and press **<Enter>**. Note that not only the data changes to match the entry but that the chart is resized to accommodate the new data.

3. Charts created on separate sheets work in the same way. Click on the sheet **Chart**. Note that the **February Sales** are **5000** (and are more than the costs). Click on **North** and return the value in cell **D6** to **3010** by typing or with **Undo**.

4. Check back to the **Chart** sheet and note that the **February Sales** figure has changed.

5. Display the **Results** sheet and in cell **C6**, enter the formula **=North!C6+South!C6+Mid!C6**, either by typing or by pointing. This creates links to cell **C6** in each regional sheet to produce a consolidated value.

6. Use the **Fill handle** to copy the formula into **D6** to **F6**. Note that relative addressing is still maintained across the sheets.

7. In **C7** enter **=SUM(North:Mid!C7)**. This is a **3D SUM** function, unlike the formula in **C6**.

continued over

Driving Lesson 43 - Continued

[i] *3D-sum can also be entered using the **AutoSum** button, then selecting the required cell in the **North** sheet, holding down <Shift> and clicking the **Mid** sheet tab.*

8.   Copy this formula into **D7** to **F7**.

[i] *To enter links to single cells, **Copy** and **Paste Link** can be used.*

9.   Click cell **H2** in sheet **North** and click the **Copy** button on the **Home** tab in the **Clipboard** group.

10.   Click cell **B3** in sheet **Results**, from the **Paste** drop down select **Paste Link**. This pastes a link to the Manager's name from sheet **North**, not just its current value.

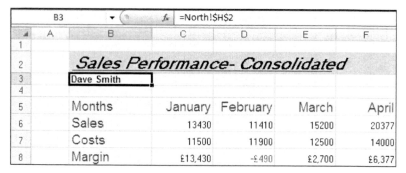

11.   On sheet **North** enter your own name in **H2** as Manager. Switch to sheet **Results** and the name will have been changed.

12.   Change any **Sales** or **Cost** data on the regional sheets and the change will be reflected immediately in the charts and on the **Results** sheet.

13.   Close the workbook <u>without</u> saving.

Driving Lesson 44 - Linking Between Workbooks

▣ Park and Read

Links created between workbooks include the source workbook name as well as the sheet and the cell reference, e.g. **=[budget.xls]Sheet1!C10**. Links are best created with the workbooks open.

If after creating a link the source workbook is closed, then the cell reference formula will also include the full location of the file, e.g.

=C:\...\...Documents\Excel 2010 Data\[budget.xlsx]Sheet1!B7.

To create links between workbooks, copy from the source document and paste into the destination document using the **Paste Link** option.

Charts are simply copied from one workbook and pasted into another.

Always save the source workbook first.

⌒ Manoeuvres

1. Open the workbook **Sales**.

2. Click on the chart and copy it.

3. Start a new blank workbook and with the active cell as **A1**, paste the chart. The chart is linked automatically back to **Sales**.

4. In the **Sales** workbook, change the value in cell **C5** to **200000** and note the change in the new workbook.

5. Close both workbooks <u>without</u> saving and start a new blank workbook.

6. In **A1** enter **Source Document**, in cell **B3** enter a number and save the workbook as **Source**.

7. Start a new workbook. In cell **A1** enter **Container Document** and then save it as **Container**.

8. Display the two worksheets side by side by selecting **Arrange All** from the **View** tab. Choose the **Vertical** option and click **OK**.

9. Make **D5** active (point and click) in **Container**.

10. Create a link by typing **=** and make the **Source** workbook active and click on cell **B3**. Press **<Enter>** to complete the formula. Display the contents of cell **D5** in the **Container** document, which should read:

    =[Source.xlsx]Sheet1!$B$3

11. In **Source**, change the number in cell **B3**. Cell **D5** changes automatically because of the link.

continued over

Driving Lesson 44 - Continued

12. Enter a list of 5 numbers starting in **B3** in **Source** down the column. Use the **AutoSum** button to total them in **B8**.

13. In cell **D5** in **Container**, type in the label **Total** to overwrite the earlier link.

14. Make **D6** the active cell in **Container**. Type **=** to start a formula and then click in the **Source** workbook to make it active then point and click on **B8** to create a link. Press <Enter> to complete the formula. The link is then created and should be;

=[Source.xlsx]Sheet1!$B$8.

 *An alternative method of linking is to use **Copy** at the source and then on the container sheet use **Paste Link** button from the **Paste** drop down to create the link.*

15. Copy the contents in cell **B5** in **Source**. Make the workbook **Container** active, click on cell **D8** and create a link, select **Paste Link**.

16. A link has now been created between **B5** in **Source** and **D8** in **Container**. Change the number in **B5**. The numbers in cells **D6** and **D8** in **Container**, and that in **B8** in **Source** change automatically.

17. Save the workbook **Container** and close it.

18. In the **Source** workbook, change two of the numbers in the list and note the total.

19. Save and close the **Source** workbook.

20. Open the **Container** workbook. The original value is still shown in **D8**. The first time the workbook is opened a warning message is displayed.

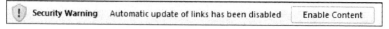

21. Click **Enable Content**. The link is updated and **D8** shows the amended value retrieved from the **Source**.

22. Close the **Container** workbook <u>without</u> saving so that the amended value is not saved.

23. Open the **Container** workbook again. Cell **D8** still shows the original value and a message is now displayed with a choice of updating or not.

continued over

Driving Lesson 44 - Continued

24. Although the links can be updated from here, for the purposes of this exercise click **Don't Update**.

25. Click in cell **D8**. As the source workbook is no longer open, the link in the formula now shows the full path.

26. The links can be updated at any time. To update the links, display the **Data** tab and click **Edit Links** from **Connections**.

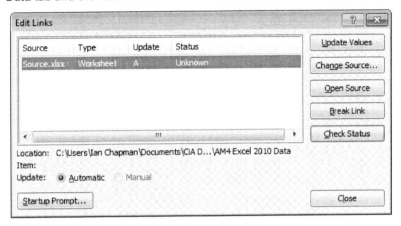

27. This dialog box controls the links in this workbook. The options are listed on the right. A link can be updated, changed or the removed. Click **Update Values**. The new total is retrieved from the unopened workbook. Click **Close**.

28. Save the workbook **Container**.

29. To break a link, select **Edit Links** and with the required link selected, click **Break Link**.

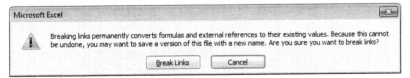

30. Read the message and then click **Break Links** to convert the cell to its existing value.

31. The link is removed. Click **Close** to close the **Edit Links** dialog box.

32. Click in cell **D8**. Only the current value is displayed in the formula, the link path is permanently lost.

33. Close the **Container** workbook <u>without</u> saving.

Driving Lesson 45 - Linking to a Word Document

🄿 Park and Read

A spreadsheet created in *Excel* can be copied into a *Word* document. This can be done in such a way that the data is linked to the workbook it originated from and any changes to the original workbook are reflected in the *Word* document.

Manoeuvres

1.   Open the workbook **Sales**. This workbook contains a spreadsheet and a chart, that are to be linked to a word processed document.

2.   Start the application *Word*.

3.   In a new document, enter the text **This data is linked back to the Sales workbook**.

4.   Insert a blank line (two presses of <**Enter**>), then enter the text **Changes made will be reflected in this document**. Press <**Enter**>.

5.   Switch back to the **Sales** workbook in *Excel*.

6.   On the **Sales** sheet, select and **copy** the range **B4:E7**.

7.   Switch to the document in *Word*. Place the cursor between the two paragraphs.

8.   Select **Paste Special** from the **Paste** drop down.

9.   In the **Paste Special** dialog box select **Microsoft Excel Worksheet Object** from the **As** box. Then select the **Paste link** option.

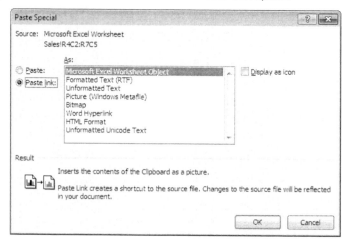

continued over

Driving Lesson 45 - Continued

10. Click **OK** to paste the range as a linked object.

11. Switch back to *Excel*, click on the chart and copy it.

12. Switch back to *Word*.

13. Move the cursor to the end of the document and select **Paste Special** from the **Paste** drop down.

14. As before select from the **As** box the **Microsoft Excel Chart Object** and select the **Paste link** option. Click **OK**. The chart is linked back to the worksheet.

15. Note that the **May** sales for the **North** region is **£150,000**.

16. Save the *Word* document as **Linked** in the **AM4 Excel 2010 Data** folder and then close it.

17. Switch to *Excel*. Change the **May** sales figure for the **North** to **£130,000** and save the worksheet using the same name.

18. Switch back to *Word* and open the document **Linked**. Click **Yes** to update the links in the document.

This data is linked back to the Sales workbook.

Company Sales	North	Central	South
May	£130,000	£110,743	£90,466
June	£140,376	£100,833	£100,744
July	£140,244	£120,500	£140,775

Changes made will be reflected in this document.

19. Both the cell in the table and the chart, have been updated to show **£130,000**. Save the document and close the *Word* application.

20. In *Excel*, change the **130000** back to **150000**.

21. Save the workbook using the same name and close it.

i *To make changes to the linked information double click to display the source data in Excel.*

Driving Lesson 46 - Hyperlinks

▣ Park and Read

When a spreadsheet is being viewed on screen, there are ways of making it easier for users to move to different locations within it, or to access connected information held in other locations. This is done using **hyperlinks**.

A hyperlink can be applied to a cell in a spreadsheet so that clicking the cell will display another location in the sheet which has been defined with a name. The hyperlink may also display a different worksheet, or open a different workbook. Alternatively the hyperlink could be used for reference purposes, opening a file from a different application or a web page.

↱ Manoeuvres

1.   Open the supplied data file **Hotel**. This is a multi sheet workbook that has had names applied to some cell ranges. Make sure the **Accounts** sheet is displayed. Some hyperlinks will be added to this sheet.

2.   Click on cell **G2**, **Profit**, select the **Insert** tab and click the **Hyperlink** button in the **Links** group.

3.   Make sure **Place in This Document** is selected from the left of the dialog box, and if necessary click the ⊞ at the left of **Defined Names** to reveal the list of available names.

4.   Select the name **Profit**. This has been defined as applying to the **Net Profit** figures, B34:N34 on this sheet. Click **OK**.

5.   Click on cell **H2**, **Rates**, and click the **Hyperlink** button. Make sure **Place in This Document** is still selected.

continued over

Driving Lesson 46 - Continued

6. The names under **Cell Reference** represent worksheet names in this workbook. Select the worksheet name **Rates** from this list and click **OK**.

7. Click on cell **I2**, **Information**, and click the **Hyperlink** button, on the **Insert** tab. Select **Existing File or Web Page** and **Current Folder**.

8. If necessary, use the **Look in** box to locate the supplied data folder then select **Notes.docx** and click **OK**.

9. Click cell **J2**, **Consultants**, and click the **Hyperlink** button. Make sure **Existing File or Web Page** is selected.

10. Type **www.ciatraining.co.uk** in the **Address** box and click **OK**.

11. On the spreadsheet move the cursor over cell **G2**, the cursor changes to a hand indicating a link. Click on cell **G2** to display the **Profit** range.

12. Click the hyperlinked text, **Rates**, in cell **H2**. The **Rates** sheet is opened.

13. Return to the **Accounts** sheet and click on cell **I2**. The **Notes** document is opened in your word processing application. Click **Yes** if a security notice is displayed. This is the incorrect document, the correct notes are stored in the document **Information**.

14. Close the word processing application and right click on cell **I2** the **Information** hyperlink. Select **Edit Hyperlink** and select the correct document **Information**. Click **OK**.

15. Check that the hyperlink displays the **2007** Notes. Close the word processing application and then click cell **J2**. If you have a live Internet connection the **CiA Training** web site will be opened in your browser.

16. Close your browser. To delete the hyperlink in cell **J2**, right click on it and select **Remove Hyperlink**. The hyperlink is deleted. Click on **J2** to check.

17. Leave the workbook **Hotel** open.

Driving Lesson 47 - Importing Delimited Data

🅿 Park and Read

Data can be imported to a spreadsheet in various formats.

Data may be imported into a workbook from a text file, as long as the text file has been saved in the correct format and the text set out in such a manner that separators (tabs, commas, spaces, etc.) can be specified to split the text into the columns.

Manoeuvres

1.   The workbook **Hotel**, should still be open. If not, open it.

2.   Click the **Insert Worksheet** tab, at the bottom of the window to insert a new worksheet. Rename the sheet **Staff** by double clicking on it.

3.   Click in cell **A1** of the **Staff** worksheet then on the **Data** tab, from the **Get External Data** group click, From Text.

4.   Ensure that within **Import Text File**, the folder containing the supplied data is displayed. Ensure that the **Files of type** is set to **All Files**. Select the file **People.txt** from the list and click **Import**.

ℹ️   *People.txt is a comma delimited data file which could have come from a wide range of sources. If you want to see the structure of it, open it in **Notepad**.*

5.   The **Text Import Wizard** opens. Ensure all options are set as shown. A basic preview of the data layout is shown in the lower part of the box.

continued over

Driving Lesson 47 - Continued

6.   Click **Next** to display Step 2. Ensure that the **Comma** option is checked in the **Delimiters** section. A clearer preview of the data layout is shown in the lower part of the box.

7.   Click **Next**.

8.   At Step 3 of 3 format the data in any column by selecting specific columns in the **Data preview** section and setting the required data format in the **Column data format** section. The data in all columns should be set to **General** by default. If not, correct the formats. Click **Finish**.

9.   The **Import Data** dialog box is displayed.

10. Ensure that the **Existing worksheet** option is checked and the address is **A1**. Click **OK**. The data from the text file **People.txt** is imported into the empty worksheet, starting at cell **A1**.

11. Close the workbook <u>without</u> saving.

Driving Lesson 48 - Revision: Linking & Importing

This is not an ECDL test. Testing may only be carried out through certified ECDL test centres. This covers the features introduced in this section. Try not to refer to the preceding Driving Lessons while completing it.

1. Make sure that there are no workbooks open, even a blank workbook. Open the workbooks **Hotel 2007**, **Hotel 2008**, and **Hotel 2009**.

2. The occupancy figures for single rooms are to be compared over the three year period. Open **Hotel Library**.

3. The single room bookings are all stored in **B7:M7** of the 3 source workbooks. The ranges to copy have all been named **SINGLES**. Create the necessary links to **Hotel Library**.

4. With **Hotel Library** active maximise the window. Enter the formulas to calculate % occupancy in the rows **10** to **12**, assume a **300** room per month capacity.

5. Format the range **B10:M12** as percentages to two decimal places.

6. Sum in cell **N6** all the monthly figures. Copy the formula to cells **N7** and **N8**.

7. Enter a function to average the monthly occupancy figures in cell **N10**. Copy the formula to cells **N11** and **N12**.

8. Use the print options screen to preview the worksheet. Select to print on one piece of paper and landscape. Print a copy of the worksheet.

9. Save the workbook as **Hotel Occupancy**.

10. Chart the occupancy rows as a three series **Line** chart (remember to include the month labels). Move the chart to a separate sheet.

11. Print a copy of the chart.

12. Close all the open workbooks <u>without</u> saving.

---

i   *Answers are shown in the **Answers** section at the end of the guide.*

If you experienced any difficulty completing this Revision refer back to the Driving Lessons in this section. Then redo the Revision.

Once you are confident with the features, complete the Record of Achievement Matrix referring to the section at the end of the guide. Only when competent move on to the next Section.

Section 11
Sorting

By the end of this Section you should be able to:

Sort Data

Perform Multiple Sorts

Create and Use Custom Lists

Perform Custom Sorts

To gain an understanding of the above features, work through the **Driving Lessons** in this **Section**.

For each **Driving Lesson**, read the **Park and Read** instructions, without touching the keyboard, then work through the numbered steps of the **Manoeuvres** on the computer. Complete the **Revision Exercise(s)** at the end of the section to test your knowledge.

Driving Lesson 49 - Sorting

🄿 Park and Read

Ranges of cells in a worksheet can be sorted so that the rows in the range are arranged in a specific order. The column used to control the sort is called the **Sort Key**.

🄿 Manoeuvres

1. Start a new blank workbook.

2. Enter a column of 8 names (surnames or first names) starting in cell **B3**.

3. Sort the names into ascending alphabetic order by highlighting the range to be sorted (**B3:B10**) and from the **Home** tab, **Editing** group, click **Sort & Filter** and then select **Sort A to Z**.

🄸 *Selecting the whole range to be sorted is not strictly necessary in this example but this shows the technique of sorting cells that may be part of a larger worksheet.*

4. With the range still selected, sort it into descending order using **Sort Z to A**.

5. Add ages (in years) in column **C** adjacent to the names.

6. To sort all of the data in ascending order of age, highlight the range **B3:C10** and select **Custom Sort** from the **Sort & Filter** drop down.

7. Select **Column C** from **Sort by**, **Smallest to Largest** from **Order** and click **OK** to perform the sort.

8. Close the workbook <u>without</u> saving.

Driving Lesson 50 - Multiple Column Sorts

▣ Park and Read

In a list, the records (rows) can be sorted into a specific order based on the values of one or more of the fields (columns).

To sort a list, the method is the same as for an ordinary sort, except that the data does not have to be selected prior to sorting, selecting a cell anywhere in the list will automatically sort the whole list.

↷ Manoeuvres

1. In a new workbook, enter the list information as shown in the rows and columns below, i.e. starting in cell **A6**.

	A	B	C	D	E	F	G
6	Make	Model	Reg.No	Engine	Colour	Mileage	Price
7	Austin	Maestro	YK51 LMT	1600	Silver Grey	7124	2250
8	Vauxhall	Corsa	Y19 LTJ	1300	Black	74123	1250

2. Open the workbook **Car Data**.

3. To add more data to the list, **copy** the range **A1:G10** in **Car Data** to a range starting **A9** in the workbook opened at step 1.

4. Save the workbook as **Classic Cars**.

5. Close the **Car Data** workbook.

6. Select all the data then select **Custom Sort** from the **Sort & Filter** drop down to display the **Sort** dialog box.

7. Make sure that the **My data has headers** box is checked.

8. Sort the list into ascending order by **Make**.

9. Click **Add Level** to perform a secondary sort in ascending order by **Model**.

10. The list is defined as having a header row with **Make** in the **Sort by** box and **Model** in the first **Then by** box.

continued over

Driving Lesson 50 - Continued

11.　Click **OK** to perform the sort.

12.　Use the **Undo** button on the **Quick Access Toolbar** to return the list to the original order.

13.　Insert a new **Column A** and set the column width to **3.00** units.

14.　Label the column **No** and enter **1** in cell **A7**.

15.　Select the range **A7:A18**. Using the **Home** tab, click **Fill**, , from the **Editing** group. Click to select **Series** and then click **OK**, to number each row, in order, starting with 1 up to 12.

16.　Sort by **Price** in descending order. Which car is the second cheapest?

17.　Sort the cars into ascending numeric order by **Mileage**. Which car has the most mileage?

18.　Using column **A** re-sort the range back to its original order.

ℹ️ *If records are to be returned to their original order after sorting, leading zeros may have to be added to labels that include numbers so that they sort correctly.*

19.　Save the workbook using the same file name.

20.　Close the workbook.

ℹ️ *Answers are shown in the **Answers** section at the end of the guide.*

Driving Lesson 51 - Custom Lists and Sorts

🅿 Park and Read

The normal **Sort** function will order items alphabetically or numerically, ascending or descending. It is however possible to sort data into any specified order using **Custom Lists**. Some **Custom Lists** are provided as defaults in *Excel*, others can be defined by the user.

👉 Manoeuvres

1.   Open the workbook **Invoices**.

2.   Type **Order Day** in cell **H5**, and **Tuesday** in cell **H6**.

3.   Enter a random selection of days of the week into cells **H7** to **H14** to represent the day on which each order was received. As this is a demonstration only, do not worry about matching days to the date field.

4.   A normal sort on the **Order Day** column will arrange the days in alphabetical order. To sort into weekday order, click a cell in column **H** and select **Sort & Filter** then **Custom Sort** from the **Home** tab or click the **Sort** button on the **Data** tab.

5.   Make sure the **Sort by** box shows **Order Day** and click the **Order** drop down list and select **Custom List**.

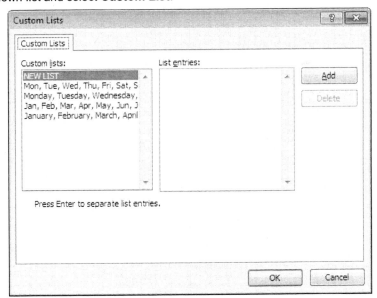

6.   Select the list starting **Monday, Tuesday** and click **OK** to return to the **Sort** dialog box.

continued over

Driving Lesson 51 - Continued

7.   Click **OK** to sort the list into weekday order.

 *Once a **Custom Sort** has been requested, the sort order will be used as the default the next time **Sort Options** is displayed.*

8.   Close the workbook <u>without</u> saving.

9.   Start a new workbook.

10.   The **Sort Options** displayed in the last diagram can be added to. This is used when a list of items is frequently used as it saves time entering them or sorting them into a non-alphabetic order, e.g. a list of employees, departments, etc. To add a user defined **Custom List**, select **Sort & Filter** then **Custom Sort**. Click the **Order** drop down list and select **Custom List**.

11.   A list is created by entering the items, with **NEW LIST** selected, enter the following list, under **List entries** (use <**Enter**> between entries):

            Director

            Manager

            Supervisor

            Administration

            Production

12.   Click **Add** then **OK**. Cancel the **Sort** dialog box. The **Custom List** is now stored and can be used.

 *Once **Custom Lists** have been added they can be used in any workbook.*

13.   In cell **A1** enter **Name** and in cell **B1** type **Status**.

14.   Create a list of at least 10 names (surname space then first name) down column **A** under **Name**. Under **Status** in column **B** add one of the five custom list entries beside each name in random order. Make sure to use each one of the custom list entries.

15.   Place the cursor in the **Status** column in the list. This data can now be sorted into the custom list order.

16.   Select **Sort & Filter** then **Custom Sort**. Click the **Order** drop down list and select **Custom List**. Select the last entry **Director**, etc, then **OK**. The list is sorted into the **Custom List** order.

17.   To delete the **Custom Lists** just created, display the **Custom Lists** dialog box and select the last entry, click **Delete**, then **OK** to confirm the deletion to remove them. Click **OK** to close the **Custom Lists** dialog box. Cancel the **Sort** dialog box.

18.   Close the workbook <u>without</u> saving.

Driving Lesson 52 - Revision: Sorting

This is not an ECDL test. Testing may only be carried out through certified ECDL test centres. This covers the features introduced in this section. Try not to refer to the preceding Driving Lessons while completing it.

1.   Open the workbook **League**.

2.   Sort the teams into alphabetic name order.

3.   **Undo** the last operation.

4.   Sort the teams into descending order of points. If the points are equal, then sort on the goal difference, again in descending order. Then sort on the number of goals-for (descending).

5.   Print a copy of the league table.

6.   Close the workbook <u>without</u> saving.

7.   Open the workbook **Supplies** which shows part of the order book for a Building Supplies Merchant.

8.   Using a **Custom Sort**, sort the records first by **Month Required** but in the order of **Jan**, **Feb**, etc. and then by ascending **Customer** name.

9.   Print a copy of the worksheet.

10. Close the workbook <u>without</u> saving.

If you experienced any difficulty completing this Revision refer back to the Driving Lessons in this section. Then redo the Revision.

Once you are confident with the features, complete the Record of Achievement Matrix referring to the section at the end of the guide. Only when competent move on to the next Section.

Section 12
Lists

By the end of this Section you should be able to:

Filter Lists using the AutoFilter

Use Custom Criteria with AutoFilter

Use the Advanced Filter

Filter using Complex Criteria

Extract Filtered Data

Add Subtotals to Lists

To gain an understanding of the above features, work through the **Driving Lessons** in this **Section**.

For each **Driving Lesson**, read the **Park and Read** instructions, without touching the keyboard, then work through the numbered steps of the **Manoeuvres** on the computer. Complete the **Revision Exercise(s)** at the end of the section to test your knowledge.

Driving Lesson 53 - Lists

🅿 Park and Read

A **List** is a labelled series of rows that contain similar information - for example a list of employees, showing their names, salaries, expenses, holidays, etc. A list can be used to:

- Search or query to find specific data.
- Sort data alphabetically or numerically by rows in ascending or descending order.
- Search for matching criteria by filtering and copying to a different part of the spreadsheet.
- Perform statistical calculations on the data for analysis and decision-making.
- Print data organised for specific purposes.

A **List** separates information into columns, each containing similar information. A row contains a set of **fields**, each defined by **field names**. A completed row is a **record**. A list is composed of many such records. The field names appear as column headings with the field information below them.

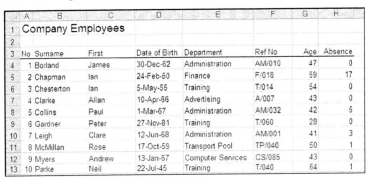

	No	Surname	First	Date of Birth	Department	Ref No	Age	Absence
	1	Borland	James	30-Dec-62	Administration	AM/010	47	0
	2	Chapman	Ian	24-Feb-50	Finance	F/018	59	17
	3	Chesterton	Ian	5-May-55	Training	T/014	54	0
	4	Clarke	Allan	10-Apr-66	Advertising	A/007	43	0
	5	Collins	Paul	1-Mar-67	Administration	AM/032	42	5
	6	Gardner	Peter	27-Nov-81	Training	T/060	28	0
	7	Leigh	Clare	12-Jun-68	Administration	AM/001	41	3
	8	McMillan	Rose	17-Oct-59	Transport Pool	TP/040	50	1
	9	Myers	Andrew	13-Jan-67	Computer Services	CS/085	43	0
	10	Parke	Neil	22-Jul-45	Training	T/040	64	1

A sample list occupying the range A3:H13.

A field containing formulas or functions is called a **computed field**.

ℹ️ *Avoid having more than one list on each worksheet. Filtering can only be used on one list at a time. The **Column** labels at the top of a list can use two rows providing the labels are formatted differently to the list, e.g. font, alignment, colour, patterns etc.*

A list follows these rules:

- The area to be used must be rectangular, although it may contain blanks.
- Use the same type of data in each column.
- Do not separate the labels from the data with a blank or decorative row.
- Do not duplicate column names and to avoid confusion they should be different from any range names.
- Enter all the list information across each row.

Driving Lesson 54 - Filtering Lists

▣ Park and Read

Filtering is a quick way to find records in a list that match search criteria. Only the rows that match are displayed. The rows that do not match are hidden, not deleted.

There are two ways to filter a list: the **AutoFilter** (for a simple filter) and the **Advanced Filter** (for more complex filtering). When a list is filtered, the worksheet is placed in **Filter Mode**.

*A worksheet in **Filter Mode***

In **Filter Mode**, the labels at the top of the list columns contain drop down arrows. If one of these arrows is clicked, a list of all different values in the column is revealed. The filter to be applied can then be selected from the list.

The default view is to show all rows **(Select All)**, until an alternative selection is made from the **Text Filters** list. Other options include:

Sort A to Z	to sort the list into ascending order
Sort Z to A	to sort the list into descending order
Sort by Color	where criteria can be applied and data can be compared via **Custom Sort**.

In the example above, all members of staff in the **Catering** department can be displayed by un-checking **(Select All)** and checking **Catering** from the drop down list for **Department**.

Driving Lesson 55 - AutoFilter

▣ Park and Read

AutoFilter produces a subset of a list with the click of a button. This places the worksheet in **Filter Mode**. Click on any of the arrows to display a drop down list of unique values in that column. Click on any item and the matching records (rows) will be displayed with the other rows hidden.

AutoFilter always selects from the whole list. **AutoFilter** can be applied to selected columns in a list by selecting them before entering **Filter Mode**.

🗺 Manoeuvres

1. Open the workbook **Sick**.

2. Enter **Filter Mode** by clicking on a cell in the list and then in the **Data** tab, within the **Sort & Filter** group, click the **Filter** button, | Filter |.

3. Using the **Surname** drop down list, scroll down the list, un-check **Select All**, check **Smith** and click **OK**. Only the Smiths are displayed.

5				
6	Surname ⏷	Initial ⏷	Department ⏷	Abse ⏷
12	Smith	F	Finance	1
13	Smith	John	Production	4
21	Smith	James	Production	2
29	Smith	C	Training	4
30				

> ℹ *The drop down arrows are displayed as, ⏷, if active with a filter applied.*

4. To redisplay the full list using the **Surname** drop down list, check **(Select All)** at the top of the list and click **OK**.

5. Exit **Filter Mode** by selecting the **Filter** button again.

6. Open the workbook **Survey** and click on any cell in the list.

7. Enter **Filter Mode**.

8. To display all the males from Sunderland who have replied, select **M** from **Sex**, **Sunderland** from **Town** and **1** from **Reply**.

9. To redisplay the whole list, instead of checking **Select All** from the three lists, click **Clear**, ⌧ Clear in the **Sort & Filter** group. All filter selections are removed.

> ℹ *A filtered list can be printed.*

10. Click **Filter** to exit **Filter Mode**.

11. Close the workbook **Survey** <u>without</u> saving and leave the workbook **Sick** open.

Driving Lesson 56 - Custom AutoFilter

🅿 Park and Read

Custom AutoFilter allows more complicated details than a simple information match. Two conditions for selecting values within the same column can be applied by using any of the 12 options (equals, is less than, etc.). **Custom AutoFilters** can be applied both to **numbers** and **text** columns.

🢅 Manoeuvres

1.   The workbook **Sick** should still be open. If not, open it.

2.   Using the workbook **Sick**, enter filter mode by clicking on a cell in the list and then in the **Data** tab, within the **Sort & Filter** group, click the **Filter** button.

3.   Click on the **Absent** drop down list and select **Number Filters**.

ℹ️   *Simple searches can be carried out using one set of criteria. More complicated filters can be carried out using either **And** or **Or** then add another set of criteria.*

4.   To display all the employees who have had less than five days absence, select **Less Than** from the list. The **Custom AutoFilter** dialog box is displayed. Enter **5** in the **Information** box.

5.   Click **OK**. The drop down of **Absent** is displayed as, 🔽, showing that a filter has been applied. To restore the list, click on the **Absent** field drop down list and check **Select All** and click **OK**.

6.   To display all the employees in either the **Administration** or **Computer Services** departments use the **Custom AutoFilter**, within the **Department** field, with the **equals** and the **or** options.

7.   Click **OK** to complete the filter. Only the records for the **Computer Services** and **Administration** are displayed.

8.   Exit **Filter Mode** by clicking the **Filter** button.

9.   Leave the workbook **Sick** open for the next Driving Lesson.

Driving Lesson 57 - Advanced Filtering

🅿 Park and Read

To search a list for more complex criteria, e.g. matching information from two fields rather than one, **Advanced Filter** can be used. This involves setting up a **Criteria Range** in a separate range of cells, normally to the top or right of the list. The **Criteria Range** consists of at least 2 rows, the column headings for the list, and one or more rows directly underneath to enter the **selection criteria**. Once this has been set up, then the list can be filtered.

A **Criteria Range** can also be arranged to combine two searches by placing information on the same row (combination '**and**') or on two rows (combination '**or**'). If the same name is required for an 'and' combination the field name must be duplicated.

🖐 Manoeuvres

1. Open the workbook **Sick**, if not already open.

2. To create a criteria range, copy the field names **A6:D6** and paste to cell **A1** (**Copy** and Paste are found on the **Home** tab or right click for a shortcut menu).

> ℹ️ *Copying the field names results in fewer mistakes being made than by typing. Also, copying all the names means that other filters can be performed using the same range.*

3. To setup a search for all the staff in administration with less than 5 days absence, on row **2** enter **Administration** under **Department** and **<5** under **Absent**.

	A	B	C	D	E
1	Surname	Initial	Department	Absent	
2			Administration	<5	
3					
4					
5					
6	Surname	Initial	Department	Absent	
7	Chapman	I	Finance	17	
8	Waldram	B	Computer Services	2	
9	Parr	N	Training	1	
10	Myers	A	Computer Services	0	
11	Westgarth	S	Catering	0	

Criteria Range A1:D2

> ℹ️ *The criteria range must be at least one column and two rows. The first row contains the field names in any order. The other rows contain the required selection criteria for the filter.*

4. The criteria range is now set up for the filtering to take place. Select a cell in the main list and in the **Data** tab, click the **Advanced** button, 🟡 Advanced from the **Sort & Filter** group.

continued over

Driving Lesson 57 - Continued

5. The **List range** has been automatically defined and is correct. Click in the **Criteria range** box and select the range **A1:D2** (it could have been **C1:D2**, as this is all that is being used but using the larger range means that other filtering can be done later with other fields without redefining the criteria range).

6. Leave the other options as they are and click **OK** to filter the list in-place.

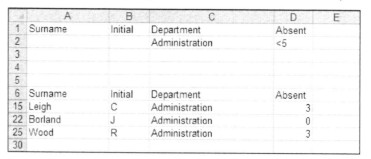

	A	B	C	D	E
1	Surname	Initial	Department	Absent	
2			Administration	<5	
3					
4					
5					
6	Surname	Initial	Department	Absent	
15	Leigh	C	Administration	3	
22	Borland	J	Administration	0	
25	Wood	R	Administration	3	
30					

7. Return to the full list using the **Clear** button, 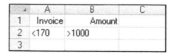.

8. Try another **and** filter by clearing row **2** and entering new search criteria.

9. Close the workbook <u>without</u> saving.

10. Open the workbook **Invoices**.

11. To filter the list using the **Invoice** and **Amount** fields, copy those two field names from row **5** to row **A1** and **B1** to set up the **Criteria range**.

12. To find invoice numbers less than 170 and amounts of more than £1000 excluding VAT, enter **<170** below **Invoice** and **>1000** below **Amount**.

	A	B	C
1	Invoice	Amount	
2	<170	>1000	
3			

continued over

Driving Lesson 57 - Continued

13. Select a cell in the list and click the **Advanced** button.

14. Click in the **Criteria range** box and select the range **A1:B2** on the worksheet. Click **OK** to filter the list.

5	Invoice	Date	Co. No.	Company	Amount	VAT	Total
8	167	21-Dec-06	345	J Jones	£1,345.00	£235.38	£1,580.38

15. There should only be one record. Click the **Clear** button to remove the filter.

16. The last example was of an **and** search. To find the invoices dated before 1st Jan 2007 or totals over 750, an **or** search is needed. Delete the range **A1:B2** and create the following criteria range:

	A	B
1	Date	Total
2	<1/1/07	
3		>750

17. Using **Advanced Filter** and the **Criteria Range** as **A1:B3** (to include the extra row) display the matching records (there should be **6**).

18. Click on a cell in the list and click **Clear**.

19. Delete the data from the range **A1:B3**.

20. A more difficult search would involve, for example, **Amounts** between £300 and £500 (note these values exclude VAT). This is an **and** search (on the same line) but the field name has to be given twice. Create the criteria range as shown right. (**AutoFilter** can do the same task and is easier).

	A	B
1	Amount	Amount
2	>300	<500

21. Use the **Advanced Filter** to display the matching records.

5	Invoice	Date	Co. No.	Company	Amount	VAT	Total
6	156	3-Dec-06	378	Greens	£456.00	£79.80	£535.80
9	168	21-Dec-06	387	CIA Training Ltd	£345.50	£60.46	£405.96
14	176	13-Jan-07	198	Car Mart	£378.00	£66.15	£444.15

22. Remove the filter.

23. Delete the data from the range **A1:B2**.

24. Leave the workbook **Invoices** open for the next Driving Lesson.

Driving Lesson 58 - Extracting Filtered Data

▣ Park and Read

Extracting means copying the filtered records that match the criteria to another part of the worksheet. All the field names need not be used, so that specific information for a specific purpose can be extracted to form another list. The original list remains unaffected.

↱ Manoeuvres

1. The workbook **Invoices** should still be open. If not, open it.

2. Copy the range **A5:G5** and paste to cell **A1**. In cell **G2** enter **<1000** to find all the small amounts owed.

3. Select a cell in the list and display the **Data** tab. Click the **Advanced** button from the **Sort & Filter** group.

4. Select **A1:G2** as the **Criteria range**.

5. Select the **Copy to another location** option.

6. Click in the **Copy to** box and then click on cell **A20**.

7. Click **OK**. The matching records are placed in a range starting **A20**.

8. Delete the range **A20:G25**.

9. Only a part of the same list is to be extracted: **Invoice**, **Company** and **Total**. Copy the three field names one at a time to the range **A20:C20**.

10. Select a cell in the list then select the **Advanced Filter**, **Copy to another location** and in the **Copy to** box add the range **A20:C20**.

11. Click **OK** to extract the matching records. Only fields for the selected headers are extracted.

12. Close the workbook <u>without</u> saving.

Driving Lesson 59 - Adding SubTotals

Park and Read

Data in a **List** can be automatically summarised, producing subtotals based on any column. The list must first be sorted on the column for which subtotals are required. **Subtotals** are then automatically inserted on each break within that column, as well as a **Grand Total** for the whole column. Although the **SUM** function is usually used in subtotals, other functions such as **COUNT** or **AVERAGE** can be used.

When subtotals are added an **Outline View** of the list is produced grouping the data rows. This outline can be manipulated, for example to hide the detail rows and show only the subtotals.

Manoeuvres

1. Open the workbook **Sick**.

2. To display a total for the days absent, subtotalled by **Department**, first sort the list by column **C**, the **Department** column into ascending order.

3. Select a cell in the list and then in the **Data** tab, **Outline** group, select **Subtotal** to display the **Subtotal** dialog box.

4. Click in the **At each change in:** box and select **Department**.

5. Click in the **Use function:** box to see the possible options, but leave it set to **Sum**.

6. Make sure that in **Add subtotal to:** there is a check in the **Absent** box.

continued over

Driving Lesson 59 - Continued

7. Leave the other options as shown and click **OK**. The list is now displayed with **Absent** subtotals for each **Department**, a **Grand Total** at the end, and an **Outline view** of the list to the left of the worksheet area.

1 2 3		A	B	C	D
	5				
	6	Surname	Initial	Department	Absent
	7	Leigh	C	Administration	3
	8	Collins	P	Administration	5
	9	Borland	J	Administration	0
	10	Wood	R	Administration	3
	11	Wilson	D	Administration	34
	12			**Administration Total**	45
	13	Clarke	A	Advertising	0
	14			**Advertising Total**	0
	15	Westgarth	S	Catering	0
	16			**Catering Total**	0
	17	Waldram	B	Computer Services	2
	18	Myers	A	Computer Services	0
	19	Waterman	D	Computer Services	7
	20			**Computer Services Total**	9
	21	Chapman	I	Finance	17
	22	Smith	F	Finance	1
	23			**Finance Total**	18
	24	Phillips	L	Personnel	2
	25			**Personnel Total**	2
	26	Smith	John	Production	4
	27	Smith	James	Production	2
	28	Barrett	N	Production	7
	29			**Production Total**	13
	30	Parr	N	Training	1
	31	Wright	B	Training	4
	32	Chesterton	I	Training	0
	33	Smith	C	Training	4
	34			Training Total	9

Outline View (label pointing to outline area at rows 13-14)

8. The **Outline** view shows that there are three levels in this list, **1=Grand Total**, **2=Department** subtotal, **3**=full detail. By default, all levels are displayed on the worksheet. Click on the **Level 2** button at the top of the outline view to collapse level 3 and only show subtotals.

9. Click on the **Level 1** button to collapse subtotals and only show the grand total. Individual groups may be collapsed and expanded by clicking their **Hide** buttons ⊟, or **Show** buttons ⊞.

10. Click the **Show** button ⊞, for the **Grand Total** to expand back to subtotals. Click the **Show** button for the **Production Total** to expand that group only.

11. Click the **Level 3** button to expand all levels again.

12. To remove the **Subtotals** select **Subtotal** from the **Outline** group on the **Data** tab and click the **Remove All** button.

13. Close the workbook <u>without</u> saving.

Driving Lesson 60 - Revision: Lists

This is not an ECDL test. Testing may only be carried out through certified ECDL test centres. This covers the features introduced in this section. Try not to refer to the preceding Driving Lessons while completing it.

1. Open the workbook **Staff**.

2. Display the **AutoFilter** and filter the list to display only the employees in the **Computer Services** department.

3. Display all the records.

4. Filter the list to show the employees between **40** and **50** years old inclusive.

5. Remove the **AutoFilter**.

6. Insert **3** more rows under row **1**.

7. Copy the field names to row **3**.

8. Use the **Advanced Filter** to extract a record of the employees in the **Administration** department, starting at cell **A30**.

9. Print a copy of the workbook.

10. Close the workbook <u>without</u> saving.

 *Answers are shown in the **Answers** section at the end of the guide.*

If you experienced any difficulty completing this Revision refer back to the Driving Lessons in this section. Then redo the Revision.

Once you are confident with the features, complete the Record of Achievement Matrix referring to the section at the end of the guide. Only when competent move on to the next Section.

Section 13
Pivot Tables

By the end of this Section you should be able to:

Understand PivotTables

Create a PivotTable

Update a PivotTable

Filter, Group and Sort Data in a PivotTable

To gain an understanding of the above features, work through the **Driving Lessons** in this **Section**.

For each **Driving Lesson**, read the **Park and Read** instructions, without touching the keyboard, then work through the numbered steps of the **Manoeuvres** on the computer. Complete the **Revision Exercise(s)** at the end of the section to test your knowledge.

Driving Lesson 61 - PivotTables

▣ Park and Read

A **PivotTable** organises and then summarises large amounts of data from any range that has labelled columns. Typically, two of the fields from the original data can act as the row and column headings for the new table. A third can optionally be used to group the tables into separate pages. **PivotTables** are created by default on a separate worksheet but can be created on the same sheet by entering a starting cell reference that does not overlap with the original base data.

↱ Manoeuvres

1. Open the workbook **Survey**.

2. Click inside the list and from the **Insert** tab, **Tables** group, select **PivotTable**.

3. The **Create PivotTable** dialog box is displayed. The **Table/Range** is selected correctly. The **PivotTable** is to be created on a **New Worksheet**. Click **OK**.

4. A blank **PivotTable** is placed on a new sheet with the **PivotTable Field List** displayed. Two new **Ribbon** tabs are added **Options** and **Design**. under **PivotTable Tools**.

continued over

Driving Lesson 61 - Continued

5.   **Fields** are dragged from the **PivotTable Field List**, to the PivotTable areas. Drag **Town** to the **Row Labels** section and **Sex** to the **Column Labels** section.

6.   To summarise data into area by the sex of the people in the survey, drag the **Town** field on to the $\sum$ **Values** area. The default calculation for text fields is **Count**.

7.   The **PivotTable** is created. The data items are a count of the people surveyed, organised by town and sub divided into males and females.

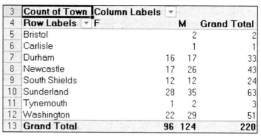

3	Count of Town	Column Labels		
4	Row Labels	F	M	Grand Total
5	Bristol		2	2
6	Carlisle		1	1
7	Durham	16	17	33
8	Newcastle	17	26	43
9	South Shields	12	12	24
10	Sunderland	28	35	63
11	Tynemouth	1	2	3
12	Washington	22	29	51
13	Grand Total	96	124	220

8.   Click on the sheet away from the **PivotTable**, the **PivotTable Field List** is hidden. Click inside the **PivotTable** and the **PivotTable Field List** is re-displayed.

9.   To organise the table differently the fields can be changed round, i.e. pivoted. Change **Town** and **Sex** over by dragging the buttons to each other's area. Observe the changes then return **Town** and **Sex** to their original positions.

10. Go back to the **Survey Results** sheet and make some changes to **Town** fields (people have moved house).

11. The **PivotTable** is now out of date, click on **Sheet1**, the sheet containing the PivotTable and then click inside the table. **PivotTables** do not automatically update, under **PivotTable Tools**, in the **Options** tab, **Data** group, click the **Refresh** button.

i   *An alternative method to update a **PivotTable** is with the active cell inside the table, right click and select **Refresh**.*

12. Save the workbook as **Survey2** and leave it open for the next Driving Lesson.

Driving Lesson 62 - Filtering a PivotTable

▣ Park and Read

A single data item can be displayed in a **PivotTable** by dragging a field to the **Report Filter** area and then using a drop down list to select it. More specific filtering is done using the **Row Labels** drop down inside the PivotTable. The fields required to be displayed are checked.

↱ Manoeuvres

1. The workbook **Survey2** should be open. If not, open it.

2. Drag the **Town** field from the **Row Labels** area to **Report Filter**.

3. Click on the drop down arrow next to **All**, at the top of the sheet to select an area to display.

4. Select **Sunderland** and click **OK**.

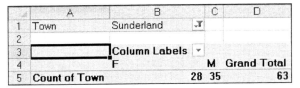

5. Select another **Town** from the drop down list.

6. Drag the **Town** field from the **Report Filter** back to the **Row Labels** area.

7. Specific information can be displayed or hidden. Click the **Row Labels** drop down. All the towns are checked.

8. Click on the **South Shields** tick to uncheck it.

9. Click **OK**. The information for **South Shields** is hidden.

10. Redisplay the information for **South Shields** by repeating the above and either checking **Select All** or adding the check to **South Shields**.

11. Leave workbook **Survey2** open.

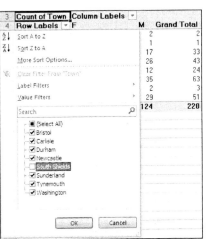

Driving Lesson 63 - Grouping and Sorting in PivotTables

▣ Park and Read

As well as displaying data summarised by any of the columns in the original list, **Pivot Tables** can be also be used to further arrange items into new groups. For example, with data summarised by month, January, February and March can be further grouped into Quarter1; or with data grouped by town, selected towns can be grouped to form Region 1.

Once data has been grouped, the original detail can be hidden so that only the group totals are shown.

☞ Manoeuvres

1. If the workbook **Survey2** is not open, open it now and display the sheet containing the **PivotTable**, if not already shown.

2. Sorting is performed in PivotTables in a similar way to lists. Place the cursor in the **Grand Total** column and click the **Sort Smallest to Largest** button, ⬇️, from the **Options** tab in the **Sort & Filter** group. The values are sorted.

3. With the active cursor still in the **Grand Total** column, click the **Sort Largest to Smallest** button, ⬆️.

4. To return the **PivotTable** to its original state, place the cursor in the **Town** column and click the **Sort A to Z** button, ⬇️. The towns are sorted into ascending alphabetic order.

5. The town data can be manually grouped into regions. Click to select **Durham**, hold down the <Ctrl> key, and click on **Sunderland** and **Washington** in Column **A**, then release <Ctrl>.

6. Select **Group Selection** from the **Options** tab to create a group containing those towns.

7. The group will be named **Group1** by default. Click on the name and change it to **Wearside**.

8. Define another group containing **Newcastle**, **South Shields** and **Tynemouth** and call it **Tyneside**.

9. Select any remaining towns and group them under the name **Other**.

continued over

Driving Lesson 63 - Continued

	Count of Town	Column Labels ▼		
3				
4	Row Labels ↓↑	F	M	Grand Total
5	⊟Other			
6	Bristol		2	2
7	Carlisle		1	1
8	⊟Wearside			
9	Durham	16	17	33
10	Sunderland	28	35	63
11	Washington	22	29	51
12	⊟Tyneside			
13	Newcastle	17	26	43
14	South Shields	12	12	24
15	Tynemouth	1	2	3
16	Grand Total	96	124	220

The numbers shown reflect the original data, your changes will have altered these values.

10. The groups can be collapsed. Click **Wearside** and then click ⊟ to hide the detail rows within the **Wearside** group.

i *Alternatively, double clicking a group name, e.g. **Wearside**, will toggle between Hide and Show data for that group.*

i *Grouping Data and Hiding/Showing detail is exactly the same for columns as for rows.*

11. A **PivotTable** can be amended, the row, column or count data can be changed. To change the count data to replies from the town, drag **Count of Town** out of the **Values** area and drag **Reply** into the **Values** area.

	Count of Reply	Column Labels ▼		
3				
4	Row Labels ↓↑	F	M	Grand Total
5	⊟Other			
6	Bristol		1	1
7	Carlisle		1	1
8	⊟Wearside			
9	Durham	5	6	11
10	Sunderland	11	13	24
11	Washington	10	6	16
12	⊟Tyneside			
13	Newcastle	4	7	11
14	South Shields	6	3	9
15	Tynemouth		2	2
16	Grand Total	36	39	75

*The PivotTable displays those who have replied by **Town** and by **Sex**.*

12. Replace the **Count of Reply** with **Count of Town** in the ∑ **Values** area.

13. PivotTables can also be automatically grouped by adding an extra field. Click on **Town2** and drag it out of the **Row Labels** area to remove it.

continued over

Driving Lesson 63 - Continued

14. Drag the **Surname** field to below **Town** in the **Row Labels** area and the people are then grouped by their town. Check down the list.

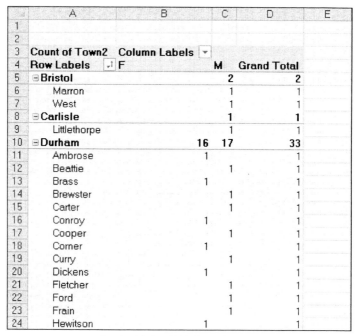

	A	B	C	D	E
1					
2					
3	**Count of Town2**	**Column Labels** ▼			
4	**Row Labels** ⬇	**F**	**M**	**Grand Total**	
5	⊟ **Bristol**		2	2	
6	Marron		1	1	
7	West		1	1	
8	⊟ **Carlisle**		1	1	
9	Littlethorpe		1	1	
10	⊟ **Durham**	16	17	33	
11	Ambrose	1		1	
12	Beattie		1	1	
13	Brass	1		1	
14	Brewster		1	1	
15	Carter		1	1	
16	Conroy	1		1	
17	Cooper		1	1	
18	Corner	1		1	
19	Curry		1	1	
20	Dickens	1		1	
21	Fletcher		1	1	
22	Ford		1	1	
23	Frain		1	1	
24	Hewitson	1		1	

Sample of the PivotTable Grouped by Town

15. Close the workbook <u>without</u> saving.

Driving Lesson 64 - Revision: PivotTables

This is not an ECDL test. Testing may only be carried out through certified ECDL test centres. This covers the features introduced in this section. Try not to refer to the preceding Driving Lessons while completing it.

1. Open the workbook **Staff**.

2. Create a **PivotTable** on a new sheet, making sure that the **Table/Range** contains the cell range of the whole table.

3. Use **Department** as the row field and **Surname** as the values field to give a breakdown of manpower by department.

4. Insert a row into the original list (not at the end) and add your own details, assigning yourself to **Production**, ref number **P/041** and **0** absence.

5. Refresh the **PivotTable** to see the effect.

6. Print the **PivotTable**.

7. Amend the **PivotTable** by removing the **Count of Surname**, adding **Age** as the **Column** field and **Absence** as the new ∑ **Values** field.

8. Group the data into the following Age Groups; **Under 40**, **40 - 50**, and **Over 50**. Which age group is responsible for the most absences?

9. Print a copy of the amended **PivotTable**.

10. Close the workbook <u>without</u> saving.

*Answers are shown in the **Answers** section at the end of the guide.*

If you experienced any difficulty completing this Revision refer back to the Driving Lessons in this section. Then redo the Revision.

Once you are confident with the features, complete the Record of Achievement Matrix referring to the section at the end of the guide. Only when competent move on to the next Section.

Section 14
Functions

By the end of this Section you should be able to:

Use Date and Time Functions

Use Lookup Functions

Use Mathematical and Statistical Functions

Use Financial Functions

Use Text and Database Functions

Use Nested Functions

To gain an understanding of the above features, work through the **Driving Lessons** in this **Section**.

For each **Driving Lesson**, read the **Park and Read** instructions, without touching the keyboard, then work through the numbered steps of the **Manoeuvres** on the computer. Complete the **Revision Exercise(s)** at the end of the section to test your knowledge.

Driving Lesson 65 - Functions

🅿 Park and Read

Functions are specialised formulas that make calculations easier. They are grouped into categories, and some of the more common functions are listed here, grouped into the appropriate categories:

Statistical	COUNT, COUNTA, COUNTIF
Financial	NPV, FV, PMT, RATE, IRR
Logical	IF, OR, AND, TRUE, FALSE
Math & Trig	SUMIF, ROUND
Text	CONCATENATE, LOWER, PROPER, UPPER
Date & Time	TODAY, DAY, MONTH, YEAR, DATE, NOW, TIME
Database	DSUM, DMIN, DMAX, DCOUNT
Lookup & Reference	HLOOKUP, VLOOKUP

In general:

Statistical functions deal with analysing numerical data, from simple counting and averaging to calculating complex distribution parameters.

Financial functions deal mainly with calculations involving depreciation, loan repayments and investments over extended time scales.

Logical functions deal with the testing and setting of conditions involving **TRUE** or **FALSE** values.

Math & Trig functions deal with processing individual numerical data, from simple rounding to complex trigonometric calculations.

Text functions deal with manipulating text strings.

Date and Time functions deal with the processing and reformatting of all data relating to dates and times.

Database functions deal specifically with data, usually numeric, held in a list or database.

Lookup & Reference functions deal mainly with data in tables or ranges, for example, retrieving values or transposing vertical and horizontal ranges.

Functions, like formulas, are preceded by an = sign.

Functions can be used as values in calculations.

Functions can be used within other functions (nested functions).

Other spreadsheet applications may have different names for the same functions.

Driving Lesson 66 - Date and Time Functions

▣ Park and Read

Dates and times are stored as numbers of days since 00:00 on 1st Jan 1900. Calculations using dates and times are carried out using the numbers which represent the dates and times. There are two key presses which automatically insert the current date and time.

<Ctrl ;>   Inserts the current date as text.

<Ctrl Shift ;>   · Inserts the current time as text.

There are also several functions for use purely with dates and times.

DATE   Returns the number for a particular day, e.g. DATE(92,4,13) returns 33707, the number of days from 1st Jan 1900 to 13th Apr. 1992.

DAY, MONTH,YEAR   Converts a date to a number representing the day, month, or year, e.g. DAY("23/11/67") would be 23.

NOW   Used as NOW(). Returns the current date and time as a number, and is updated as the worksheet is calculated.

DATEVALUE   Converts the date as text to a number, e.g. DATEVALUE("21-Sept-49") returns 18162.

TODAY   Used as TODAY(). Returns the current date as a number and is updated as the worksheet is calculated.

WEEKDAY   Converts a number to an integer representing the day of the week from 1 (Sunday) to 7 (Saturday), e.g. WEEKDAY("21-Sept-49") returns 4, Wednesday.

TIME   Used as TIME(hour,minute,second). Returns a value in the range 0 to 0.99999999, representing a fraction of a day, e.g. TIME(16,48,10) returns 0.700115741.

TIMEVALUE   Returns a number as a fraction of the day, e.g.TIMEVALUE("22nd-Aug-67 6:35 am") returns .274305556.

HOUR, MINUTE,SECOND   Converts a time into hours, minutes, or seconds, e.g. HOUR("6:35pm") returns 18.

continued over

Driving Lesson 66 - Continued

Manoeuvres

1. Open a new workbook. This Driving Lesson shows some of the described functions in action.

2. In **B2**, enter the label **Time as number**. In **D2**, enter **Time as text**.

3. In **B4**, enter **=NOW()** and format it to display as **hh:mm:ss**. In the **Home** tab, **Number** group, and from the **General** drop down select **Time**.

4. In **D4**, press **<Ctrl Shift ;>** to enter the current time.

5. In **B8**, enter the function **=TIME(8,30,0)** and custom format to display as **hh:mm**.

6. In **B12**, enter **=B4-B8** to calculate an elapsed time. Format the value as **Time**.

7. The **Time as number** and **Time as text** should now appear as different times. This is because the function **NOW()** is updated as the worksheet is calculated, while using **<Ctrl Shift ;>** puts text in the sheet, which is not updated.

8. In **F2**, enter **=TODAY()**.

9. In **F4**, enter **=DATE(** then your date of birth as numbers in the form **yy,mm,dd** followed by a **)**.

10. In **F8**, enter **=F2-F4**. Format the cell as a number with no decimal places. This shows your age in days.

11. In **H4**, enter **=WEEKDAY(F4)**. This gives a number corresponding to the day of the week on which you were born (Sunday = 1, Saturday = 7). Add a **Custom** format to cell **H4** of **dddd**.

12. In **J4** enter **=DAY(F4)** to extract the day part of your birth date.

13. In **J5** enter **=MONTH(F4)** to extract the month part of your birth date.

14. In **J6** enter **=YEAR(F4)** to extract the year part of your birth date.

15. Close the workbook <u>without</u> saving.

Driving Lesson 67 - Lookup Functions

P Park and Read

The **Lookup** functions are used to look up relevant data from a table, to use in a calculation. There are two functions, **HLOOKUP**, which searches a horizontal table and **VLOOKUP**, which searches a vertical table.

A **Lookup** table consists of a selection of bands, or intervals, within which a given value can be found.

Manoeuvres

1. Open the workbook **Discount**. The worksheet consists of a discount calculation at the top and two lookup tables at the bottom, one a horizontal and one vertical, containing the same data. The discount to be used (in **D8**) depends directly on the number of items bought.

2. To look up the discount from the horizontal table using the **HLOOKUP** function, click in cell **D8**.

3. Click the **Lookup & Reference** button on the **Formulas** tab, in the **Function Library** group and select the function **HLOOKUP**.

i   *Alternatively, click the **Insert Function** button in the **Function Library** group or in the **Formula Bar** then proceed to the **Insert Function** dialog box as used in previous versions of Excel to select functions.*

4. The **Lookup_value** is cell **D4** (number bought). The **Table_array** is **C14:I15** (the table without the labels) and the **Row_index_num** is **2** (to return the value from the 2nd row of the table).

continued over

Driving Lesson 67 - Continued

*Setting the **Range_lookup** to **FALSE** causes the function to return a value only if there is an <u>exact</u> match between the **Lookup_value** and the table entry. Leave it blank here.*

5.   Click **OK**.

6.   The value returned is **10%**, corresponding to selling between 5 and 9 items.

▲	A	B	C	D	E
1	**Lookup Tables**				
2					
3	Price			£69.95	
4	Number Bought			5	
5					
6	Total Price			£349.75	
7					
8	Discount %			10%	
9	Discount			£34.98	
10	Discount Price			£314.78	
11					

7.   Change the number bought in **D4** to **23**. The **Discount %** changes, and so does the **Discount Price**.

8.   Delete the contents of cell **D8**.

9.   To use the **VLOOKUP** function on the vertical table, click in cell **D8**.

10. Click the **Lookup & Reference** button and select the function **VLOOKUP** (this function is similar to **HLOOKUP** except the base data is stored in columns).

11. The **Lookup_value** is cell **D4** (number bought). The **Table_array** is **B19:C25** (the table without the labels) and the **Col_index_num** is **2** (to return the value from the 2nd column of the table).

12. Click **OK** to complete the function.

13. Change the number bought in **D4** to **52**. The **Discount %** changes to **45%** the **Discount Price** is **£2000.57**.

14. Close the workbook <u>without</u> saving.

Driving Lesson 68 - Mathematical Functions

P **Park and Read**

SUMIF only sums values within a range that match a set condition, e.g. to sum the outstanding amounts of clients that owe more than £100.

ROUNDUP and **ROUNDDOWN** can be used to round a numeric value to any number of figures either up or down.

Manoeuvres

1. Open the workbook **Invoices**.

2. In cell **D17**, enter the label **Small invoices total**.

3. Select cell **E17** and click the **Math & Trig** button in the **Formulas** tab.

4. Scroll down the list and select the **SUMIF** function.

5. The **Function Arguments** box for **SUMIF** is displayed. Select the **Range** as **E6:E14** and enter the **Criteria** as **<500**. Click **OK**.

6. To show the invoice totals rounded down to the nearest pound, enter **Round Down** in H5 then select cell **H6**.

7. Click the **Math & Trig** button. Select the function **ROUNDDOWN**.

8. Select the **Number** as **G6**. Set the number of digits in the **Num_digits** box as **0**. Click **OK** to insert the function. The invoice total is shown rounded down to the nearest pound.

9. Copy the function in **H6** to fill the range **H7** to **H14**.

10. The customer would benefit from rounding down. **ROUNDUP** raises the amount higher to the specified level, usually to the next pound. Enter **Round Up** in cell **I5** then select cell **I6**.

11. Select the **ROUNDUP** function. Select the **Number** as **G6** and set the number of digits in the **Num_digits** box as **0**. Click **OK** to insert the function. The invoice total is shown rounded up to the nearest pound

12. Copy the function in **I6** to fill the range **I7** to **I14**.

13. Experiment with **ROUNDUP** and **ROUNDDOWN** functions by using numbers other than 0 in the **Num_digits** box (try using 2, 1,-1 and -2 to see the effects in the **Function Arguments** box).

14. Leave the workbook open.

Driving Lesson 69 - Statistical Functions

Park and Read

COUNTIF counts numeric items that match a set condition. COUNTBLANK counts the number of blank cells in a range. RANK.EQ displays a number's position in a list (values with the same rank returns the top rank of that set).

Manoeuvres

1. The workbook **Invoices** should still be open. If not, open it.

2. In cell **D16** enter the label **Invoices under £500**.

3. Select the range **E6:E14**. Click the **Define Name** button, in the **Defined Names** group on the **Formulas** tab.

4. **Amount** is suggested as the name for the range, click **OK**. The range of amounts is now named **Amount** and can be used in the function.

5. Select cell **E16**, click the **More Functions** button, click **Statistical** and then select the function **COUNTIF**.

6. The **Function Arguments** box for **COUNTIF** is displayed. In the **Range** box either type **Amount** or click and drag the range **E6:E14**. The range name is shown in the box.

7. Set the criteria in the **Criteria** box as **<500**.

8. Click **OK**. Check the **Formula Bar** for the formula (the speech marks are added automatically to the criteria). The cells that match the condition are counted. The result should be **4**.

continued over

Driving Lesson 69 - Continued

9.   Close the workbook <u>without</u> saving.

10. Open the workbook **Survey**. The function **COUNTBLANK** can be used to calculate the number of people who have not replied to the survey.

11. In cell **F227** enter **Not Replied**.

12. Click in cell **G227**, click the **More Functions** button, click **Statistical** and then select the function **COUNTBLANK**.

13. Select the **Range** as **G6:G225**.

14. Click **OK**. The function counts the blank cells, i.e. the people who have not replied. The answer displayed is **145**.

15. The **RANK** function orders the values in a range and displays a number's position in the list, for example, the last person in the list, is he the oldest person surveyed? In cell **H225** enter **Ranked by age**.

16. Make sure that the label is left aligned.

17. Click in cell **J225**, click the **More Functions** button, click **Statistical** and then select the function **RANK.EQ**.

18. Select **E225** as the **Number** (the last person in the list) and select the **Ref** as **E6:E225** the range of all the ages.

19. Click **OK**. The function ranks the selected age and displays **9**. Therefore there are eight older people surveyed in the list.

20. Close the workbook <u>without</u> saving.

Driving Lesson 70 - Text Functions

🅿 Park and Read

The ampersand symbol, **&**, or the **CONCATENATE** function can be used to connect the contents of two or more cells that contain text. Other text manipulation functions are used to extract parts of text entries. **LEFT** extracts characters from the left, **RIGHT** extracts characters from the right, **MID** extracts characters from the middle (starting position and number of characters) and **TRIM**, used to tidy up data entry by removing space from an entry leaving only one space between words.

Manoeuvres

1. Open the workbook **Strings**.

2. On the **Strings** sheet, in **G4**, enter the formula **=A4&B4&C4**. The words in these cells are joined together, but with no spaces.

3. In **G5**, enter the function **=A5&" "&B5&" "&C5**. Each set of speech marks is around one space. This adds the spaces between the text.

4. The function **CONCATENATE** can be used to achieve the same result. In **G6**, enter the formula **=CONCATENATE(A6," ",B6," ",C6)** to achieve exactly the same effect as step 3.

ℹ️ *Entering a function directly avoids the need to select a function and use the* ***Function Arguments*** *dialog box. It is quicker providing you know the arguments that are required.*

5. Copy **G6** up to **G5** and **G4**.

6. The **Ref No.** is to be made up of the initials of the customer added to the invoice number. In **F4** enter the function **=LEFT(B4,1)&LEFT(C4,1)&D4**. This gives an individual reference number.

7. Copy the formula in **F4** down to **F5** and **F6**.

8. The stock list in cell **A11**, **0543BW00521** is made up of a part number (first 4 characters), the initials of the person who checked it (the next 2 characters) and the amount in stock (the last 5 characters).

9. In cell **B11**, enter the formula to extract the first 4 characters, the part number **=LEFT(A11,4)**. Press **<Enter>**.

10. In cell **C11**, enter the formula to extract the initials of the person who checked the item **=MID(A11,5,2)**, this starts at the 5th character and extracts 2 characters. Press **<Enter>**.

continued over

Driving Lesson 70 - Continued

11. In cell **D11**, enter the formula to extract the last 5 characters, number of items in stock **=RIGHT(A11,5)**. Press **<Enter>**.

12. In cell **A15** is an example of a driving licence. In cell **B15** use the **MID** function to extract the date of birth. The day is characters **9** and **10**. The month is characters **7** and **8**. The year is character **6** and **11**.

13. The date of birth should be **29/05/36**. Copy the formula to cell **B16**. What is this date of birth?

14. Display the **Text** sheet. This shows a small list of names where spaces have been captured in error. To tidy the display the **TRIM** function can be used.

15. In cell **C4** enter the function **=TRIM(B4)**.

16. Copy the function from **C4** down the column to cell **C12**.

17. To see the effect of **TRIM** in greater detail, the range **B4:B12** has been copied to the starting cell **B15**. Highlight the range **B15:B23**, display the **Home** tab, click **Find & Select** and then **Replace**.

18. In the **Find what** box, enter a space and in the **Replace with** box enter a hash **#**.

19. Click **Replace All**, click **OK** and then close the dialog box. This shows where the spaces were.

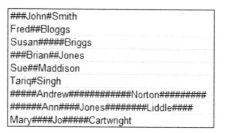

```
###John#Smith
Fred##Bloggs
Susan#####Briggs
###Brian##Jones
Sue##Maddison
Tariq#Singh
#####Andrew############Norton#########
#####Ann####Jones########Liddle####
Mary####Jo#####Cartwright
```

20. Close the workbook <u>without</u> saving.

i *Answers are shown in the **Answers** section at the end of the guide.*

Driving Lesson 71 - Financial Functions

🅿 Park and Read

Three of the many financial functions deal with the repayment of loans. If **pv** is the present (original) value of the loan, **rate** is the interest rate per period, **nper** is the total number of payments and **pmt** is the repayment per period, the following functions can be used.

=PMT(rate,nper,pv).   Calculates repayments if **rate**, **nper** and **pv** are known.

=RATE(nper,pmt,pv).   Calculates the rate if **pmt**, **nper** and **pv** are known.

=PV(rate,nper,pmt,).   Calculates the loan value if **rate**, **pmt** and **nper** are known.

Similar functions deal with the results of investing or saving:

=FV(rate,nper,pmt)   Calculates the final value of saving an amount **pmt** for **nper** periods at **rate** percent interest.

=NPV(rate,value1,value2,..)   Calculates the net present value of an investment using a comparison discount rate of **rate** and a series of future income payments (positive values) and payments (negative values).

🫱 Manoeuvres

1. Open a new workbook in which a loan repayment is to be calculated.

2. In **C2** enter the label **LOAN ANALYSIS**.

3. In **C4** enter **Interest Rate**.

4. In **C6** enter **Term (months)**.

5. In **C8** enter **Loan Amount**.

6. In **E4** enter the interest rate as **6%**.

7. The **Term** is the length of the loan. Enter **360** into **E6** (30 years).

8. In **E8** enter the size of the loan, **£50000**.

9. In **C10**, enter the label **Monthly Repayment**.

10. In **C11**, click the **Financial** button from the **Function Library** group of the **Formulas** tab and select the payment function **PMT**.

continued over

Driving Lesson 71 - Continued

11. Complete the dialog box as below:

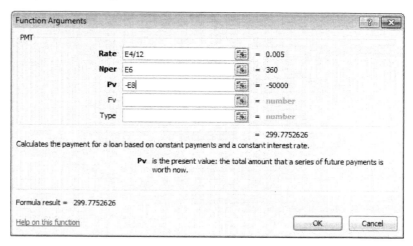

12. The **Rate** is divided by 12 to obtain a monthly rate, and the **Amount** is entered as negative because the loan is an amount owed. Click **OK** to complete the function.

13. Change the interest rate to **8%**.

14. If the maximum affordable repayment is **£300**, the maximum loan value can be calculated using **PV**.

15. In **G4** enter **8%**, in **G6** enter **360** and in **G10** enter **300**.

16. In **G8** enter the function **=PV(G4/12,G6,-G10)** to see the maximum amount that can be borrowed.

17. To see the result of investing the same amount of money under the same conditions, in **I8** enter the function **=FV(G4/12,G6,-G10)**.

18. Save this workbook as **Loan Analysis**.

19. Close the workbook.

*Answers are shown in the **Answers** section at the end of the guide.*

Driving Lesson 72 - Database Functions

▣ Park and Read

There are functions especially designed to be used with lists. The functions perform calculations on fields in a list, but <u>only</u> on those records which meet the selection conditions defined in the criteria range. For example, in a list of sales by city, database functions can be used to obtain values for a specific city only, by selecting that city in the criteria range. The available functions are as follows:

Function	Results
DAVERAGE	Averages numbers
DCOUNT	Counts numbers
DCOUNTA	Counts nonblank cells
DGET	Extracts a single value
DMAX	Finds a maximum value
DMIN	Finds a minimum value
DPRODUCT	Multiplies numbers
DSTDEV	Calculates standard deviation of a sample
DSUM	Adds numbers
DVAR	Calculates variance of a sample

↱ Manoeuvres

1. Open the workbook **Survey**.

2. To find information about people who have replied to the survey, copy the top line of the list, the titles, to row **2**. Rows **2** and **3** will be the area (criteria range) where the selection criteria for the functions will be set.

3. Enter **1** in **G3**, under **Reply** (only include records where **Reply** = '**1**').

4. In **I2** enter the label **Replies**, in **I4**, **Oldest**, in **I6**, **Youngest**, in **I8**, **Total** and in **I10**, **Average**.

5. Select the cell **J2** and click **Insert Function** button on the **Formulas** tab.

ℹ️ *Note that there is not a direct button to the **Database** functions from the **Ribbon** as with all the other types of function.*

continued over

Driving Lesson 72 - Continued

6. The **Insert Function** dialog box is displayed. Choose the category **Database** and the function **DCOUNT** from the list. Click **OK**. The **DCOUNT** dialog box is then displayed.

7. In **Database** enter **A5:G225**, in **field** click on **G5**.

8. In the **criteria** box, point or enter **A2:G3**.

9. Click **OK** to display the total number of replies.

10. Follow the same procedure to find the oldest person to reply. In **J4** enter = **DMAX(A5:G225,E5,A2:G3)**. Check the age field to confirm the answer.

11. In **J6** enter **=DMIN(A5:G225,E5,A2:G3)**. This displays the age of the youngest person to reply. Check the age field to confirm the answer.

12. In **J8** enter **=DSUM(A5:G225,E5,A2:G3)**. This displays the total age of all persons who have replied.

13. In **J10** enter **=DAVERAGE(A5:G225,E5,A2:G3)**. This displays the average age of all persons who have replied.

14. Close the workbook <u>without</u> saving.

i *Some of the answers in this Driving Lesson are rather vague as the worksheet contains the **Now** function to calculate ages from dates of birth. Everyone is getting older by the day, therefore the sum of their ages and the average age are increasing day by day.*

i *Answers are shown in the **Answers** section at the end of the guide.*

Driving Lesson 73 - Nested Functions

🄿 Park and Read

Individual functions can be combined with each other to form more complex functions. When one of the values within a function is itself a function, this is known as a **Nested Function**. An example of nested text functions is **=UPPER(LEFT(B2,3))**, which would return the upper case of the left three characters in the cell **B2**.

A common use for nested functions is in the **IF** function, where the logical test, e.g. **A1>10** within **=IF(A1>10,"Yes","No")** could be replaced by another function, e.g. **AND(A1>10,A1<20)** for greater control.

It is vital that the nested function returns a value of the same type as required by the first function or an error will result. In the first example, **LEFT** returns a text field, which is required for the **UPPER** function; and in the second example, **AND** returns a logical value (TRUE or FALSE) which is required as the first value for the **IF** function.

🄿 Manoeuvres

1.   Open the workbook **Employees**.

2.   It is decided to pay a £15 bonus to all employees 40 or over who have had less than 2 days absence this year.

3.   Enter the label **Bonus** in cell **G1**.

4.   Select cell **G2** and click the **Logical** button from the **Formulas** tab and select the function **IF** to display the **IF** box.

5.   In the **Logical_test** field enter the function **AND(E2>=40,F2<2)**.

6.   Enter **15** in the **Value_if_true** field and **0** in the **Value_if_false**.

7.   Click **OK** to complete the function.

8.   Copy the nested functions from **G2** to the range **G3** to **G20** to see who qualifies for the bonus.

9.   Print a copy of the list.

10. Close the workbook <u>without</u> saving.

ℹ️ *Answers are shown in the **Answers** section at the end of the guide.*

Driving Lesson 74 - Revision: Functions

This is not an ECDL test. Testing may only be carried out through certified ECDL test centres. This covers the features introduced in this section. Try not to refer to the preceding Driving Lessons while completing it.

1. Open the workbook **Employees**, insert four rows at the top of the sheet and copy the column headers to the new **Row 1**.

2. In **F26** use the **COUNTIF** function to calculate the number of staff over 40 years. Manually check the age column. Add the label **COUNTIF** to E26.

3. In **F27** calculate the same value using the **DCOUNT** function. Use **rows 1** and **2** as the **Criteria** range. Add the label **DCOUNT** to cell **E27**.

4. In **F28** use the **DAVERAGE** function to find the average age of staff over 40. Add the label **DAVERAGE** to cell **E28**.

5. In **F29** use the **ROUND** function to display the average age from **F28** to the nearest whole number. Add the label **ROUND** to cell **E29**.

6. Without altering the functions, find the **DCOUNT** and **DAVERAGE** values for staff over 30.

7. Create the lookup table and use **HLOOKUP** to calculate an attendance bonus (**Bonus 1**) in **Column G** based on; 0-1 days absence, £50; 2-3 days, £30, 4-5 days, £15 and 6 or more days, £0.

Absence	0	2	4	6
Bonus	£50	£30	£15	£0

   (When copying a **HLOOKUP** function down a column, remember to use absolute addressing for the lookup table.)

8. In **Column H** calculate a stress bonus (**Bonus 2**) which is **£100** for all staff in Finance or Training and **£20** for everyone else, using the **IF** function with a nested **OR** function.

9. Format **Column I** as numeric with 0 decimal places. In this column use the **YEAR** function to find the year of birth for each staff member and add 65 to it. Name the column **Retirement Year**.

10. In **Column J** use the **CONCATENATE** function to join together **First name** and **Surname** with a space between them. Widen the cells to fit the largest name and name the column **Full Name**.

11. Save the workbook as **Employees2** and then close it.

[i] *Answers are shown in the **Answers** section at the end of the guide.*

If you experienced any difficulty completing this Revision refer back to the Driving Lessons in this section. Then redo the Revision.

Once you are confident with the features, complete the Record of Achievement Matrix referring to the section at the end of the guide. Only when competent move on to the next Section.

Section 15
Charts

By the end of this Section you should be able to:

Add and Remove Data Series

Change Chart Types

Change Chart Axis Scales

Create Combination Charts

Add Images to Charts

To gain an understanding of the above features, work through the **Driving Lessons** in this **Section**.

For each **Driving Lesson**, read the **Park and Read** instructions, without touching the keyboard, then work through the numbered steps of the **Manoeuvres** on the computer. Complete the **Revision Exercise(s)** at the end of the section to test your knowledge.

Driving Lesson 75 - Formatting Charts

P Park and Read

All parts of a chart, including the colours, axes, text, gridlines, background, etc., can be changed.

Manoeuvres

1. Open the workbook **Charts**.

2. Click on the **Sales Chart** sheet tab to display the chart that has been moved to a separate sheet, then click anywhere on the chart to select it.

3. Move the cursor over the left axis of the chart, until the **ToolTip** reads **Vertical (Value) Axis**. Click to select the vertical axis.

i *Alternatively, to select any part of a chart, click the **Chart Elements** drop down on the **Format** tab in the **Current Selection** group and select the required part, e.g. **Vertical (Value) Axis**.*

4. On the **Format** tab, in the **Current Selection** group, click **Format Selection** to display the **Format Axis** dialog box.

continued over

Driving Lesson 75 - Continued

5.   With the **Axis Options** displayed, edit the value in the **Minimum** box, by checking **Fixed** and typing **2500** in the **Value** box.

6.   Change the **Maximum** to **7500** and the **Major unit** to **500** to alter the values on the axis.

7.   The chart changes dynamically as the values are completed. Move the dialog box to the right to see more of it.

8.   The values are quite large and could have been millions. The **Value Axis** can be changed to display the figures in various formats without changing the source data. In the dialog box under **Axis Options** click the drop down of the **Display units** box.

9.   The available options are displayed. Select **Hundreds** from the list.

10. Change the display to **Thousands** (large numbers could have been displayed in millions, billions, etc.). Click **Close**.

continued over

Driving Lesson 75 - Continued

11.   Display the **Layout** tab and click **Data Labels** from the **Labels** group.

12.   Various options are available to add labels to the series. Select **More Data Label Options**. Make sure that the **Value** option is checked. Note that the values match the axis display that was changed earlier.

13.   The values are added to the **Outside End** by default. Under **Label Position** select **Inside End**.

14.   Click **Close**.

15.   The chart title is **Sales** at the top centre. Click on the title and select the text. Use the **Home** tab to change the **Font Color** to **blue** and the **Font Size** to **20**.

16.   Display the **Format** tab and add a **light yellow** shaded background using the **Shape Fill** button.

17.   Add a dark blue border using the **Shape Outline** button.

18.   To reposition the chart title, click on the edge of the title, the cursor changes to a four pointed arrow and drag slightly to the left.

19.   To add a **Legend** to the chart, on the **Layout** tab, **Labels** group, click the **Legend** button. Select **Show Legend at Right**. The legend is displayed on the chart.

 *Greater control of the **Legend** positioning can be achieved using the **More Legend Options** found at the bottom of the list.*

20.   Reposition the legend further up, away from the columns, using the same click and drag method used to move the chart title.

 *A **Legend** is removed either by selecting it and using the **Delete** key or by clicking the **Legend** button and selecting **None**.*

21.   Leave the workbook open for the next lesson.

Driving Lesson 76 - Modifying Charts

🅿 Park and Read

As well as formatting the components of a chart, the chart type may be modified either globally or for individual data series. Individual data series may be removed from a chart, although this does not affect the original source data.

🏁 Manoeuvres

1. The workbook **Charts** should still be open. If not open it.

2. Make the **TvS Chart** sheet active. Select the chart, without selecting a data series. On the **Design** tab, in the **Type** group, click **Change Chart Type**.

3. The current option is displayed, i.e. **3-D Clustered Column**. Select the first option, **Clustered Column** to change the chart type from 3D to 2D. Click **OK**.

4. Click the **Turnover** data series (blue), making sure all columns are selected and click **Change Chart Type**.

5. Select the chart style **Line with Markers**. Click **OK**. Now one data series is shown as columns and one as a line chart.

6. Very carefully position the cursor on the line of the **Turnover** data series.

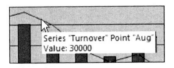

7. Right click to display a shortcut menu.

8. Select **Delete** from the resulting menu to remove the series from the chart.

ℹ️ *Alternatively, on the **Design** tab, **Data** group, click **Select Data**. Select the series to delete, and click the **Remove** button. Click **OK** to close the dialog box.*

continued over

Driving Lesson 76 - Continued

9.　Display the **Sales Chart**. Another **Data Series** can be added after a chart has been created.

10.　To add the **Profit** figures as a series, display the **Design** tab, click **Select Data**. Click **Add**. With the cursor in the **Series name** box, display the **Source Data** sheet and click on the series label **A11** (the profit label).

11.　In the **Series values** box, highlight the entry, display the **Source Data** sheet and select the series **B11:M11**. Click **OK**. The extra data series has been added to the chart. Click **OK** again to close the dialog box.

12.　The **Legend** is on display and is expanded to include the extra series. The new series is not displayed fully as some of the values are lower than **2500**, the minimum value set previously. Change the **Minimum** to **-2500**, using the **Axis Options** dialog box.

13.　To remove the series just added, an alternative method to using the **Delete** key is to display the **Select Data Source** dialog box (see step 10). Highlight the **Profit** series in the **Series** box and click the **Remove** button. Click **OK** to close the dialog box.

14.　Change the **Minimum** back to its previously set value of **2500**.

15.　Display the **TvS Chart** and change the **Chart Type** for the **Spending** data series to **Pie Chart**.

16.　Click once on the chart to select all segments, each segment has a handle.

17.　Drag any segment out from the centre. The whole pie chart will be exploded.

18.　Push any segment back to reform the chart.

19.　With the pie chart still selected, click again on a single segment to select it. This one segment can now be dragged out and pushed back.

20.　Close the workbook <u>without</u> saving.

Driving Lesson 77 - Line-Column Charts

P Park and Read

More than one data set can be represented on one chart to show a comparison of information. If required, each set of data on the chart can be shown in a different form, e.g. one set as columns and another set as a line. This is a **Line - Column** chart. If the two sets of data are for different types of data, e.g. temperature and rainfall, each set can have a different vertical axis.

Manoeuvres

1. Open the workbook **Climate**. This spreadsheet shows the rainfall and temperature for each month of the year in various cities.

2. To plot London's rainfall and temperature on a single chart, highlight the range of cells **A4:C16** containing all the necessary labels and data, then display the **Insert** tab, click the **Column** button in the **Charts** group and select a **2-D Clustered Column**.

3. Click the **Move Chart** button, select the **New sheet** option then click **OK** to place the chart on a separate sheet named **Chart1**.

4. Select the **Temperature** series (red columns) and change the chart type to a **Line with Markers**.

5. Select the **Line** and click the **Format Selection** button on the **Format** tab to display the **Format Data Series** dialog box.

6. Under **Series Options** select **Secondary Axis**. Click **Close**.

*The axis on the left shows **Rainfall** in cm and the axis on the right shows **Temperature** in degrees C*

7. Using the **Layout** tab, add **London Weather** as the **Chart Title**, **Month** as the **Horizontal Axis Title**, **Rainfall (cm)** as a the **Primary Vertical Axis Title** (rotated) and **Temperature** as the **Secondary Vertical Axis Title** (rotated).

8. Save the workbook as **Climate2** and close it.

Driving Lesson 78 - Adding Images to Charts

⯃ Park and Read

The use of images can greatly enhance the impact of charts. They can be used with any component of the chart but in practice they are most commonly used as backgrounds (the **Plot Area**, **Chart Area**) or as data columns (**Data Series**).

⮎ Manoeuvres

1. Open the workbook **Charts**.

2. Make the **Sales Chart** active.

3. Click to select <u>all</u> data columns (**Series "Sales"**) and right click and select **Format Data Series**.

4. In the **Series Options** section reduce the **Gap width** to approximately 100% by dragging the **Gap Width** slider slightly to the left.

5. In the **Fill** section, select the **Picture or texture fill** option and then click the **File** button under **Insert from**.

6. Find the image **Sales.gif** within the data files folder and double click or click and **Insert** to retrieve it.

7. Make sure that the **Stretch** option is selected, this makes the one image fill the column. Click **Close** to see the full effect on the chart.

ℹ️ *Images are added to **Bar Charts** in exactly the same way.*

8. Repeat the steps to add **Symbol.gif** and set the **Format** option to **Stack**.

continued over

Driving Lesson 78 - Continued

9. Click **Close** to see a different style of graphic representation.

10. Use **Format Data Series** dialog box and **Fill** to reset the columns to a single colour using the **Solid fill** option.

11. Use **Format Data Series** dialog box and **Series Options** to widen the gap between columns to **150** (this reduces the width of the columns). Leave the dialog box open.

12. To see the effect of an image as background, click on the **Plot Area** of the chart. The dialog box reflects the change.

13. In **Fill** select **Picture or texture fill** and click the **Clip Art** button under **Insert from**.

14. Insert any piece of **Clip Art**.

15. Click **Close**. The image fills the whole of the plot area.

16. Repeat the process and remove the **Clip Art** from the **Plot Area** by selecting the **No fill** option.

17. Insert a piece of **Clip Art** in the **Chart Area**.

 *The **Transparency** option can be used to tone down an image if it overpowers the chart.*

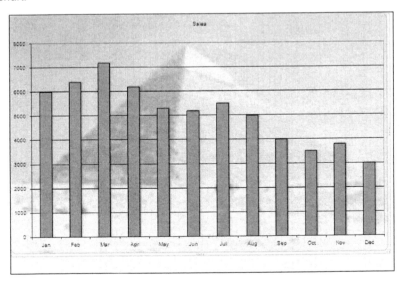

*An example of an image inserted in the **Chart Area** with **50%** transparency*

18. Close the workbook <u>without</u> saving.

Driving Lesson 79 - Revision: Charts

This is not an ECDL test. Testing may only be carried out through certified ECDL test centres. This covers the features introduced in this section. Try not to refer to the preceding Driving Lessons while completing it.

1.   Open workbook **Hotel** and delete the blank row **3**.

2.   Select the range **A3:M5** and produce a **2D column chart** for the selected data series.

3.   Add a chart a title '**Room Bookings**' and move the chart to a new sheet, using the **Move Chart** button on the **Design** tab.

4.   Click and drag the chart title into a space in the upper left of the chart area. Click and drag the legend to the upper right.

5.   Select the **Vertical Value Axis**. Change the scale of the **Minimum** value to **1000**. Display **Thousands** and format the numbers with **0** decimal places.

6.   Select the **Plot Area** and apply a light coloured textured background.

7.   Select one set of data columns and change the gap width to approximately **70%**. This should widen both data series columns.

8.   Select the **Double Room** data series and change the chart type to a line chart for that series only.

9.   Right click the line chart and remove it.

10.   Select the remaining data series and add **Data labels**. Format the labels to include the **Category Name**.

11.   Remove the **Legend**.

12.   Set the page orientation to **Landscape**, if not already set, check the print preview and then print a copy of the chart.

13.   Change the chart type to a **Pie in 2-D** chart.

14.   Select only the segment for **August** and drag it out from the rest to explode it.

15.   Close down the workbook <u>without</u> saving.

If you experienced any difficulty completing this Revision refer back to the Driving Lessons in this section. Then redo the Revision.

Once you are confident with the features, complete the Record of Achievement Matrix referring to the section at the end of the guide. Only when competent move on to the next Section.

Section 16
Data Tables

By the end of this Section you should be able to:

Create a One Input Data Table

Create a Two Input Data Table

To gain an understanding of the above features, work through the **Driving Lessons** in this **Section**.

For each **Driving Lesson**, read the **Park and Read** instructions, without touching the keyboard, then work through the numbered steps of the **Manoeuvres** on the computer. Complete the **Revision Exercise(s)** at the end of the section to test your knowledge.

Driving Lesson 80 - One Input Data Table

Park and Read

A **Data Table** is used to see how changing one variable in a formula affects the result of that formula, e.g. "How do the repayments on a loan change for different interest rates?" By using a **Data Table**, the calculation need only be done once and the results of numerous different rates can be seen.

Any function can be used as the starting point for a data table.

Manoeuvres

1. Open the workbook **Loan**. The calculation in **C11** shows the repayment amount for a loan, based on the values in **E4**, **E6** and **E8**. This Driving Lesson creates a **Data Table** showing how the result varies for a range of one of these values (**E4**, interest rate).

2. In **B12** enter an interest rate of **4%**.

3. Highlight the range **B12:B36** and on the **Home** tab, **Editing** group, click **Fill** and then **Series**. Enter a **Step value** of **0.0025**. Click **OK** and this enters a list of interest rates rising in ¼ percentage points.

4. Format the range **B12:B36** as percentages to **2** decimal places.

5. Highlight the range **B11:C36** (the range of the **Data Table** includes the calculated cell) and on the **Data** tab, **Data Tools** group, click **What-If Analysis** and then **Data Table**.

6. The values to be substituted are in a column, click in the **Column input cell** box. The value in the calculation which is actually changing down the column, is the interest rate, so click on cell **E4** to select it.

7. Click **OK**.

8. The table of values is automatically filled in, calculating the repayments for each of the different interest rates. Format the repayment figures, in column **C**, as **currency** (2 decimal places). Change the **Loan Amount** to **£60000**. The whole table is automatically recalculated.

9. Save the workbook as **Loan2** and leave it open for the next lesson.

Driving Lesson 81 - Two Input Data Table

🅿 Park and Read

A two-input data table is used to see how the results of a formula change as
two of the input values are varied. For instance, as well as varying the interest
rate of a loan, what effect does the length of the loan have on repayments? A
two input data table needs inputs for both the row and column of the table.

↱ Manoeuvres

1. The workbook **Loan2** should still be open, if not, open it. Change the
   Loan Amount back to **£50,000**.

2. Select and delete the existing results range **C12:C36**.

ℹ️ *Part of a **Data Table** cannot be deleted. To delete a **Data Table**, the whole
range must be selected.*

3. Cut and paste the cell **C11** to **B11**.

4. In **C11** enter **120**, this is 10 years expressed in months. Use **Fill Series**
   on the range **C11:G11**, with a step value of **60** (5 year intervals) to fill in
   the top row of the table.

5. Highlight the range **B11:G36** and on the **Data** tab, **Data Tools** group, click
   What-If Analysis and then **Data Table**.

6. In this table there are two variable inputs: a row and a column. In **Row
   input cell**, enter **E6** (the loan term). The **Column input cell** is **E4** (the
   interest rate, as before). Click on **OK**. The table is instantly completed.

7. Format the table appropriately. It is now possible to see at a glance how
   changes in interest rates **and** loan terms alter repayments. For example,
   the monthly repayment on £50,000 over 20 years at 5.00% is **£329.98**.

8. Save the workbook using the same file name (**Loan2**) and close it.

ℹ️ *This example uses the **PMT** (payment) function in the **Data Table**, but any
function can be used as the basis for an input data table.*

Driving Lesson 82 - Revision: Data Tables

This is not an ECDL test. Testing may only be carried out through certified ECDL test centres. This covers the features introduced in this section. Try not to refer to the preceding Driving Lessons while completing it.

1. Open a new workbook.

2. In **C1** enter **No. Rooms**, in **C2** enter **Charged** and in **C3** enter **Overhead**.

3. In **E5** enter **Price Charged** and in **A12** enter **Occupied**.

4. In **B8** enter **1** and using **Series**, produce the numbers **1** to **10** in the range **B8:B17**. This represents the number of rooms occupied.

5. In **C7:H7** enter the numbers **15** to **20** to represent the possible charges made for each room.

6. This table will calculate the profitability of the hotel, depending on the fixed overheads, the room charge and how many rooms are occupied. In the top left of the table, the formula for calculating the profit must be entered. In **B7** enter **=D1*D2-D3**, in **D1** enter **1**, in **D2** enter **20** and in **D3** enter **100** (the actual values in **D1** and **D2** can be left blank).

7. Create the two-input data table.

8. Format the data range **C8:H17** as currency, with negative numbers shown in red with a minus sign. Format the rest of the sheet appropriately.

9. From the table, how many rooms in the hotel must be occupied to guarantee a profit, regardless of the charge per room (within the charge range £15 to £20).

10. Change the overhead figure in **D3** to **130**.

11. At £20 per room the hotel is half full. Is it worth reducing the charges to £15 if this would mean it would be fully booked?

12. Obtain a printed copy.

13. Close the workbook <u>without</u> saving.

i *Answers are shown in the **Answers** section at the end of the guide.*

If you experienced any difficulty completing this Revision refer back to the Driving Lessons in this section. Then redo the Revision.

Once you are confident with the features, complete the Record of Achievement Matrix referring to the section at the end of the guide. Only when competent move on to the next Section.

Section 17
Macros

By the end of this Section you should be able to:

> · Understand Macros
>
> Record a Macro
>
> Run a Macro
>
> Assign a Macro to the Quick Access Toolbar

To gain an understanding of the above features, work through the **Driving Lessons** in this **Section**.

For each **Driving Lesson**, read the **Park and Read** instructions, without touching the keyboard, then work through the numbered steps of the **Manoeuvres** on the computer. Complete the **Revision Exercise(s)** at the end of the section to test your knowledge.

Driving Lesson 83 - Macros

P **Park and Read**

A **Macro** is a sequence of commands which can be recorded and then played back when required. Macros are useful for automating routine tasks, simplifying complex worksheets, creating custom menus, dialog boxes and buttons and running other applications. **Macros** are usually created by recording the actual cell and menu selections themselves as they occur.

*Once recorded, **Macros** are stored as instructions written in **Visual Basic** code. It is possible to amend **Macros**, or even create them directly, by editing this code.*

Excel has different macro security levels because of the potential threat from viruses. The default **Security Level** is set to **Disable all macros with notification**. This has to be reduced for this feature to work with the accompanying data files.

Manoeuvres

1. To work successfully with **Macros**, the **Developer** tab has to be displayed. If it is not already displayed, click the **File** tab, then click the **Options** button. In the **Customize Ribbon** section check **Developer** under **Main Tabs** on the right. Click **OK**.

2. On the **Developer** tab, in the **Code** group, click **Macro Security**.

3. The default setting is **Disable all macros with notification**. The security level will remain at this level until it is changed. Click **OK** to leave as the default.

4. Open the workbook **Hockey** (this is a workbook that already has macros attached to it, denoted by the **.xlsm** file name extension). Click **Enable Content** to allow the use of the attached macros.

5. The league table has just had some results added to it. To sort the league table, on the **Developer** tab, in the **Code** group, click **Macros** and choose **Sort_League**.

6. Click **Run** to carry out the sort. The league is sorted first by points, descending, then by goal difference and then by goals for.

7. Enter **Prepared by** and your full name in cell **A12**.

8. The command button **Print** on the worksheet has a **Print_League** macro attached. Click the **Print** button to print a copy of the league table.

9. Close the workbook **Hockey** <u>without</u> saving.

Driving Lesson 84 - Recording a Macro

⏸ Park and Read

It is important when creating a macro, that it is planned out beforehand, as *Excel* records all cell and Ribbon selections, including mistakes!

↱ Manoeuvres

1. Open the workbook **Hotel**. This workbook is to be used to store a variety of different macros.

2. This workbook has a **Print Area** set, display the **Page Layout** tab, click the **Print Area** button and select **Clear Print Area** to remove it.

3. On the **Developer** tab, in the **Code** group, click **Record Macro** to display the **Record Macro** dialog box.

4. In the **Macro name** box, enter **Name**.

5. Drop down the **Store macro in** box to see where macros can be stored.

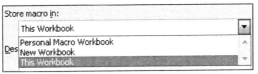

ℹ️ *For macros to be available in any workbook, they should be stored in **Personal Macro Workbook** which is always opened with **Excel** although hidden. Storing in **This Workbook** means the macro will only be available when the current workbook is open.*

6. Select **This Workbook**.

continued over

Driving Lesson 84 - Continued

 *A quick key press can be used to run a macro, but care should be taken with the letter used with **Ctrl** as this will overwrite any other function the key may have already assigned to it, e.g. <**Ctrl c**> is used for copy.*

7. Click **OK**. The **Stop Recording** button is displayed in the **Ribbon** in place of **Record Macro**. Every key press and mouse selection is now recorded.

8. You are to create a macro to customise your printouts by adding your name and other fields into the header/footer of all documents. Display the **Insert** tab and click the **Header& Footer** button.

9. Click in the **Left section** of the header and click the **Current Date** button on the **Ribbon** to insert the date field, **&[Date]**.

10. Press the <**Space**> bar on the keyboard then type **Draft**.

11. Click the **Go to Footer** button.

12. Click in the **Center section** and type your full name.

13. Click on a cell in the worksheet and then click the **Normal** button on the **View** tab.

14. Display the **Developer** tab and click the **Stop Recording** button.

15. Create a macro for changing the page orientation to landscape. Name the macro **Landscape** and store it in **This Workbook**. Use **Page Layout**, click the **Orientation** button and select **Landscape**. Display the **Developer** tab and click **Stop Recording**.

16. A macro is to be created to apply a custom number format. Click in cell **B5** and start creating a macro, name it **Format**, in the **Ctrl** box enter **f** and store the macro in **This Workbook**. Click **OK**.

17. Display the **Home** tab and click the **Number** group dialog box launcher. The **Number** tab with **Currency** is selected, change the **Decimal Places** to **0**. Click **OK** and then click **Stop Recording** on the **Developer** tab.

 *Formatting a range using **Format as Table** is inappropriate for a macro, as the feature requires a range to input during the process.*

18. Save the workbook as an **Excel Macro-Enabled Workbook (*.xlsm)** with the name **Macros** and leave it open.

 *The only way to amend a macro, <u>without</u> directly editing the **Visual Basic** code, is to record the whole sequence again.*

Driving Lesson 85 - Running a Macro

⊡ Park and Read

The macro can be activated in a variety of ways, depending on how it was set up. Some of the possible methods are covered in this Driving Lesson and the next one. Macros can be run:

- By listing the Macros and selecting from the list.
- By using a key press assigned to it.
- Adding it to the **Quick Access Toolbar** as a button and clicking on it.
- Assigning it to an object such as a box or a button on a sheet and clicking on it.

⌐ Manoeuvres

1. The workbook **Macros** should still be open, if not, open it.

2. Highlight the range **B5:N14** and on the **Developer** tab, in the **Code** group, click **Macros**.

i *The key press <Alt F8> is an alternative to the above command.*

3. Three macros have been created and are available from the current workbook. With **Format** selected, click **Run**. The cells are formatted with no decimal places.

continued over

Driving Lesson 85 - Continued

4.   Highlight the range **B17:N29** and use the key press **<Ctrl f>** to run the **Format** macro to achieve the same formatting.

 Two different ways to run a macro are described in this Driving Lesson. How you choose to run a macro depends on the application and/or your personal preferences.

5.   Open the workbook **League**, with the **Macros** workbook still open.

6.   Preview the **League Table** sheet. This worksheet has no header/footer and the orientation is **Portrait**.

7.   Click **Macros** on the **Developer** tab. All the macros created earlier are available, but only because the **Macros** workbook is still open.

 *The macro names now include the name of the workbook in which they are stored, e.g. **Macros!Format** or **Macros.xlsm!Format**.*

8.   Select the **Name** macro and run it.

9.   Check the macro effects by previewing the worksheet using the **Print** options from the **File** tab, it should contain a custom header and footer.

 There were issues in some versions of Excel 2010 which prevented macros correctly adding fields and text to headers and footers. It is not known if and when these issues will be resolved.

10. In the same workbook, run the **Landscape** macro.

11. Check the effects of the macros by previewing the worksheet, it should be in landscape orientation.

 Don't worry if the header or footer is not fully seen in landscape orientation.

12. Close the **League** workbook <u>without</u> saving.

13. Macros can easily be removed from a workbook. With the **Macros** workbook displayed, click **Macros** on the **Developer** tab.

14. Click on the name **Format** and click **Delete**.

15. Click **Yes** and the macro will be deleted.

16. Close the workbook <u>without</u> saving.

Driving Lesson 86 - Assigning a Macro to the Quick Access Toolbar

Park and Read

Macros can be added to buttons and placed on the **Quick Access Toolbar**, in any position. The **Quick Access Toolbar** is situated at the top left of the screen.

Manoeuvres

1. Open the workbook **Hockey**.

2. Click the **File** tab, then **Options** and display the **Quick Access Toolbar** section.

> The **Quick Access Toolbar** section can be opened by using the drop down arrow at the right end of the **Quick Access Toolbar** and selecting **More Commands**.

3. Select **Macros** from the **Choose commands from** box.

4. Click on the **Casual** macro and click the **Add** button. This macro changes the **Font**, **Colour** and **Italic** settings for the selected range. The default button, is displayed with the macro name. Click the **Modify** button, a different **Symbol** and **Display name** can be selected here, if required.

5. Click **OK** to leave the symbol and name unchanged.

6. The macro is placed on the **Quick Access Toolbar**. The position can be changed by clicking on an item and using the up and down arrows on the right. Move the **Casual** macro up two places. Click **OK**.

7. Test the macro by selecting the range **B4:I8** and clicking on the button on the **Quick Access Toolbar**. The cells are reformatted.

8. Open the workbook **Staff**, select the range **G4:H22** and click on the **Quick Access Toolbar**. This range is reformatted.

> The macro runs here because **Hockey** is still open. Excel will always try if possible to open the worksheet containing the macro. When assigning macros to the **Quick Access Toolbar**, it is better practice to use only macros stored in the **Personal Macro Workbook**.

9. To remove the button from the **Quick Access Toolbar**, right click on the unwanted button and select **Remove from Quick Access Toolbar**.

> Alternatively, display the **Quick Access Toolbar** section of the **Excel Options** dialog box, select the macro entry **Casual** and click **Remove**.

10. Close all open workbooks <u>without</u> saving.

Driving Lesson 87 - Revision: Macros

This is not an ECDL test. Testing may only be carried out through certified ECDL test centres. This covers the features introduced in this section. Try not to refer to the preceding Driving Lessons while completing it.

1. Open the workbook **Macro Hotel**. This workbook contains the cash flow for a small hotel.

2. In cell **A2** enter your name.

3. A printout for each quarter is required. Create a macro to print the first quarter (January to March), named **Q_one**, to be stored in **This workbook** and not to use a quick key press.

4. Run the macro **Q_one** to see if it works.

5. Create a similar macro for the second quarter (April to June), named **Q_two**.

6. Run the macro **Q_two** to see if it works.

7. Attach the **Q_one** macro to a button on the **Quick Access Toolbar** to the right of the **Save** button.

8. Click the new **Quick Access Toolbar** button to see if it works.

9. Remove the **Macro Button** from the **Quick Access Toolbar**.

10. Delete the macro, **Q_two** from the workbook.

11. Save the workbook as **Macro Revision** in a format that will support the running of macros.

12. Close the workbook.

If you experienced any difficulty completing this Revision refer back to the Driving Lessons in this section. Then redo the Revision.

Once you are confident with the features, complete the Record of Achievement Matrix referring to the section at the end of the guide. Only when competent move on to the next Section.

Section 18
Auditing

By the end of this Section you should be able to:

Use Auditing Tools

Trace Precedents and Dependents

Add and Remove Tracer Arrows

Trace Errors

Add Data Validation

To gain an understanding of the above features, work through the **Driving Lessons** in this **Section**.

For each **Driving Lesson**, read the **Park and Read** instructions, without touching the keyboard, then work through the numbered steps of the **Manoeuvres** on the computer. Complete the **Revision Exercise(s)** at the end of the section to test your knowledge.

Driving Lesson 88 - Auditing

▣ Park and Read

The **Auditing** features can be used to display the structure of calculations within a spreadsheet. They can be useful in helping to track down problems, particularly in complex worksheets with many formulas. The commands are available from the **Formulas** tab, **Formula Auditing** group.

↱ Manoeuvres

1. Open the workbook **Audit Trail**. This contains some simple formulas so that auditing techniques can be demonstrated.

2. Display the **Formulas** tab.

3. The **Formula Auditing** group controls the functions associated with auditing.

4. Place the cursor over each button in turn and check the **Tooltip**.

5. Click the **Error Checking** drop down arrow to view the other commands.

6. Click away from the menu to close it.

7. Leave the **Audit Trail** workbook open.

Driving Lesson 89 - Tracing Precedents

⊞ Park and Read

Precedents and **Dependents** are used to show the relationship between formulas and the cells that are used within them. **Precedents** are cells that are referenced by a formula in the current cell. Tracing precedents, looks at all the cells that have been used in the current formula.

⌒ Manoeuvres

1.   The workbook **Audit Trail** should still be open, if not, open it. Display the **Sales** sheet.

2.   To trace precedents for a formula, click the cell **E5** and then click the **Trace Precedents** button, [⊞ Trace Precedents], in the **Formula Auditing** group.

	A	B	C	D	E	F
1						
2		Jan	Feb	Mar	Total	
3		13	6	4	23	
4		4	1	5	10	
5		17	7	9	33	
6						

The above diagram shows the Precedents for E5

3.   With cell **E5** still selected, click the **Remove Arrows** drop down and select **Remove Precedent Arrows**. The arrow is removed.

4.   **Precedents** can also be traced to other worksheets or workbooks. Select the **Accounts** sheet and click on cell **C4** (this references **E5** on the **Sales** sheet). Click the **Trace Precedents** button, [⊞ Trace Precedents].

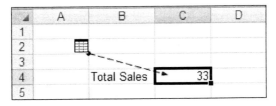

	A	B	C	D
1				
2				
3				
4		Total Sales	33	
5				

*The **Precedent** is traced to another sheet/book.*

5.   To check where the link is from, double click anywhere on the arrow.

6.   The **Go To** dialog box is displayed showing the source of the formula. To go to the source, double click on the reference in the **Go to** box. It leads back to cell **E5** on the **Sales** sheet.

ℹ️ *If the source is a different workbook it must be open, or an error is displayed.*

7.   Leave the workbook **Audit Trail** open.

Driving Lesson 90 - Tracing Dependents

▣ Park and Read

Dependents are cells that reference the current cell. Tracing dependents looks at all other cells where the current cell is used in a formula.

↱ Manoeuvres

1. The workbook **Audit Trail** should still be open, if not, open it.

2. To trace **Dependents**, click on cell **C3** on the **Sales** sheet and click the **Trace Dependents** button, ⬚ Trace Dependents .

The above diagram shows the dependents for C3, namely cells C5 and E3

3. With cell **C3** still selected, click the **Remove Arrows** drop down and select **Remove Dependent Arrows**.

4. To trace **Dependents** to other worksheets or workbooks, select cell **E5** and click the **Trace Dependents** button.

5. Cell **E5** is traced back to a linked worksheet/workbook. To check where the link is to, double click anywhere on the arrow.

6. The **Go To** dialog box is displayed showing the linked destination. Double click on the reference in the **Go to** box to go to the destination.

ℹ️ *If the destination is a different workbook it must be open, or a reference error is displayed.*

7. Click the **Remove Arrows** button, ⬚ Remove Arrows ▾ .

8. Leave the workbook **Audit Trail** open.

Driving Lesson 91 - Tracing Errors

▣ Park and Read

Auditing tools can be used to trace an error back to the source cell/s that cause the error. Tracing errors is similar to tracing precedents, but should only be used on cells that show an error value.

☞ Manoeuvres

1. The workbook **Audit Trail** should still be open, if not, open it.

2. Display the **Accounts** sheet. Cells that contain errors are displayed with a # symbol. Select cell **E11** and click the **Error Checking** drop down, `◈ Error Checking ▾` from the **Formula Auditing** group on the **Formulas** tab. Select **Trace Error**.

9	Sales Analysis				
10		Sales Achieved	Target Sales		Performance %
11		●——33—●	●	◈	►#DIV/0!
12					

ℹ️ *Selecting this option with the active cell not containing an error, results in an error message being displayed. A **Smart Tag** is displayed, `◈`, next to the cell containing the error.*

3. Double click the arrow to highlight the cell causing the error. Cell **C11** is made active. The error in **E11** is the result of the **Target Sales** cell, **C11**, not being completed.

4. **Comments** can be attached to cells that need an explanation of the contents. With cell **C11** active, display the **Review** tab and click the **New Comment** button. Enter the comment **Do not leave this cell blank**.

5. Enter **40** in cell **C11**.

6. To remove all tracer arrows, on the **Formulas** tab, click the **Remove Arrows** button, `◈ Remove Arrows ▾`. All the **Tracer Arrows** on the active worksheet are removed.

7. Display the **Sales** sheet. Cells containing errors can be identified by displaying the precedents of cells. Click in cell **H23** and display the **Precedents**. The correct range **B23:G23** is shown.

8. Click in Cell **H21** and trace the **Precedents**. The range is short, **B21:D21** as shown by a blue border. Amend the formula in **H21** to **B21:G21** the correct range. Remove all the tracer arrows.

9. Leave the workbook **Audit Trail** open.

Driving Lesson 92 - Data Validation

🅿 Park and Read

Data Validation is used to set limits to cell entries. Existing cell content that falls outside the set limits can be highlighted using the **Circle Invalid Data** command on the **Data** tab, **Data Validation** button drop down.

Manoeuvres

1. The workbook **Audit Trail** should still be open, if not, open it.

2. Select the **Validation** sheet. This worksheet contains information about orders received from companies. To make the data entry more efficient data validation can be added to some of the ranges. All the ranges displayed with a white background contain formulas and are generated automatically.

3. To add data validation, highlight the range **A4:A25** and display the **Data** tab and click the **Data Validation** button to display the **Data Validation** dialog box.

4. The **Settings** tab is displayed. In the **Validation criteria** section, display the drop down list under **Allow**.

5. Select each of the options in turn to view the changing **Data** areas.

6. Select **Whole number**. If anything is selected other than the default **Any value**, then the **Data** option displays the following **Operators**:

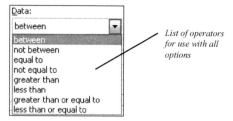

List of operators for use with all options

7. The smallest invoice number in the range is 148. Select **greater than**. Enter **147** under **Minimum**.

continued over

Driving Lesson 92 - Continued

8. Messages can be displayed to help data entry and to point out errors. Select the **Input Message** tab. The **Title** is displayed in bold above any **Input message** when the active cell is placed on a validation cell, enter **CiA Training Ltd** in the **Title** box.

9. Enter **Invoice number** in the **Input message** box.

10. Select the **Error Alert** tab. This is similar to the **Input message**, except it is displayed when the validation is not met. The **Title** is displayed in the **Title Bar** of an error message dialog box. Enter **CiA Training Ltd** in the **Title** box.

11. The type of message is selected under **Style**, from **Stop**, **Warning** or **Information** (varying strengths of control). Leave the setting as **Stop**. In the **Error message** box enter **Only whole numbers over 147**.

continued over

Driving Lesson 92 - Continued

12. Click **OK** to add the validation to the range.

13. The **Input message** is displayed as the active cell is **A4**. To test the validation click on cell **A14**. Enter an invalid invoice number, i.e. a number under 148. The **Error Alert** message is displayed.

14. Click **Retry** and enter a number over **147** but add a decimal element, e.g. **180.5**. Click **Retry** and enter a valid invoice number, **181**.

15. The next column contains the invoice date, select the range **B4:B25** and add the data validation to accept **dates greater than 1/01/08**. Add suitable messages. Click **OK**.

16. Click on cell **B14**. Test the data validation by trying an invalid date first, followed by the current date.

17. The next column contains the invoice time, office hours only between **8:30** and **17:30**. Select the range **C4:C25** and add the data validation to accept office hours only (enter the times as shown above). Add suitable messages. Click **OK**.

18. Click on cell **C14**. Test the data validation by trying an invalid time first, followed by a valid time. Remember to include a colon in a time.

19. The next column is the company number which uses the company name as a lookup. The list on the right is to be used as a list to enter the company name in column **E**. Highlight the range **E4:E25**.

20. Click the **Data Validation** button and select **List** from the **Allow** drop down in the **Settings** tab. Click in the **Source** box and highlight the list of company names on the right, **K5:K13** (the names only). Click **OK**.

21. Click on cell **E14** and click the drop down to the right. This displays a list of names from which to choose.

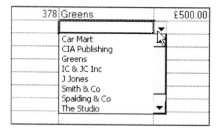

continued over

Driving Lesson 92 - Continued

22. Select a name from the list. Typing a name directly into these cells that doesn't match a name in the list results in an error message being displayed.

*Column **D** is completed automatically after selecting or typing a valid company name by using a **Lookup** table.*

23. Column **F** contains the invoice amount before VAT is added. This column can contain decimals as it is for currency. Highlight the range **F4:F25**.

24. Click the **Data Validation** button and select **Decimal** from the **Allow** drop down. Select the **greater than** operator and enter **0** in the **Minimum** box. Click **OK**.

25. In cell **F14** enter a negative value, then enter a valid number, **250.88**. The other two columns are completed automatically.

26. **Data Validation Circles** are a means of showing the cells that are outside the data validation restrictions placed on them. To display data validation circles, click the **Data Validation** button drop down and select **Circle Invalid Data**.

8	170	12-Mar-08	15:45	294	Smith & Co
9	172	15-Mar-08	17:35	187	White & Sons
10	173	21-Mar-08	11:38	202	IC & JC Inc

27. The only invalid entry is cell **C9** the out of office order (it was entered before the validation was added). Change **17:35** to **17:30** to make it valid.

*Validation circles are removed by selecting **Clear Validation Circles** from the **Data Validation** button drop down.*

28. The office hours have been extended. To edit the restrictions that are in place, highlight the range **C4:C25**, click **Data Validation**. Change the **Start** and **End times** to **8:00** to **18:00** respectively. Click **OK** to accept the changes.

*Validation is removed from cells by selecting the required range and then using the **Clear All** button in the **Data Validation** dialog box.*

29. Leave the workbook open.

Driving Lesson 93 - Revision: Auditing

This is not an ECDL test. Testing may only be carried out through certified ECDL test centres. This covers the features introduced in this section. Try not to refer to the preceding Driving Lessons while completing it.

i   *This requires the previous exercises to have been completed.*

1. The workbook **Audit Trail** should still be open. If not, open it.

2. Display the **Validation** sheet.

3. Enter a new invoice on row **14**. Invoice number **178**, invoice date **today**, in column **C** a valid time, drop the list down for the **Company** and choose **Spalding & Co** and the amount **£750**.

i   *The other three entries are all calculated from data entered.*

4. Trace the **Precedents** of cell **H8**.

5. Trace the **Dependents** of cell **F11**.

6. Trace the **Precedents** of cell **D13**. This used the company name in **Column E** and looks up the company number from the lookup table. What are they?

7. Remove the **Precedent Arrows** from cell **D13**.

8. Add your name in cell **D1**.

9. Print a copy of the range **A1:H25**.

10. Remove all the tracer arrows.

11. Save the workbook as **Auditing**.

12. Close the workbook.

i   *Answers are shown in the **Answers** section at the end of the guide.*

If you experienced any difficulty completing this Revision refer back to the Driving Lessons in this section. Then redo the Revision.

Once you are confident with the features, complete the Record of Achievement Matrix referring to the section at the end of the guide. Only when competent move on to the next Section.

Section 19
Tracking Changes

By the end of this Section you should be able to:

Track Changes in a Worksheet

Share Workbooks

Merge Workbooks

To gain an understanding of the above features, work through the **Driving Lessons** in this **Section**.

For each **Driving Lesson**, read the **Park and Read** instructions, without touching the keyboard, then work through the numbered steps of the **Manoeuvres** on the computer. Complete the **Revision Exercise(s)** at the end of the section to test your knowledge.

Driving Lesson 94 - Tracking Changes in a Worksheet

P Park and Read

If changes to a worksheet are to be retained until further consideration has been given then **Tracking Changes** can be turned on. The changes can then be accepted or rejected at a later stage.

Manoeuvres

1. Open the workbook **Budget** and save as **Tracking**.

2. To keep track of any changes that you make, display the **Review** tab, click **Track Changes** from the **Changes** group and select **Highlight Changes**.

3. Check **Track changes while editing. This also shares your workbook**.

4. Leave **When** checked as **All**.

i This action will also **Share your workbook**. *This is used in the next Driving Lesson and is used to keep track of others changing the workbook.*

5. Click **OK**.

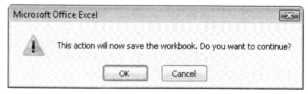

6. Click **OK** again.

continued over

Driving Lesson 94 - Continued

7.   The workbook is now shared, check the **Title Bar**.

Tracking.xlsx [Shared] - Microsoft Excel

8.   Any changes you now make will be tracked. Change **B5** to **25**.

9.   Save the workbook using the same file name **Tracking**.

10. Place the cursor over cell **B5** a comment has automatically been is attached.

	A	B	C	D	E	F	G
1	Budget	Jan	Feb	Mar	Apr	May	Jun
2	Sales	6000	6400	7200	6200	5300	5200
3	Price	6	6	6	6	6	6
4	Turnover	36000					31200
5	Workers	25	Testing1, 28/01/2010 16:07:			20	20
6	Pay	320	Changed cell B5 from '20' to '25'.			20	320
7	Wages	8000				0	6400
8	Materials	20800				0	17600
9	Overheads	5000	5000	5000	5000	5000	5000
10	Spending	33800	33800	37000	33000	29400	29000

11. Change the **September Sales** to **4500** then save the workbook using the same file name **Tracking**.

12. The changes are saved with the workbook. These changes can be listed on a separate sheet, click **Track Changes**, select **Highlight Changes** and check **List changes on a new sheet**. Click **OK**.

13. A **History** sheet is created with the changes listed. View the **History** sheet.

	A	B	C	D	E	F	G	H	I	J	K
1	Action Number	Date	Time	Who	Change	Sheet	Range	New Value	Old Value	Action Type	Losing Action
2	1	28/01/2010	16:07	Testing1	Cell Change	Budget	B5	25	20		
3	2	28/01/2010	16:07	Testing1	Cell Change	Budget	J2	4500	4000		
4											
5											
6	The history ends with the changes saved on 28/01/2010 at 16:14										

14. The changes can be reviewed at any stage by listing each one in turn and either accepting or rejecting the change. Click **Track Changes** and select **Accept/Reject Changes**.

15. Click **OK**.

continued over

Driving Lesson 94 - Continued

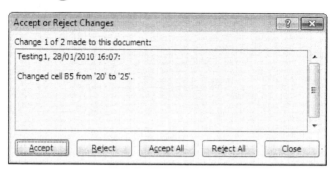

16. **Accept** the first change and **Reject** the second. The **September Sales** reverts back to **4000**.

*The comment is still attached to cell **B5** but has been removed from **J2**.*

17. Turning off the tracking, removes the workbook from shared use and the history of the changes is lost. Click **Track Changes** and select **Highlight Changes**.

18. Uncheck **Track changes while editing**.

19. Click **OK**.

20. Click **Yes** and the workbook is automatically saved and removed from shared use.

21. Close the workbook.

Driving Lesson 95 - Shared Workbooks

P Park and Read

Sharing workbooks is a way of allowing different users to update the same spreadsheet. There are two ways of doing this. The spreadsheet can be updated by different users at the same time and all the changes will be updated whenever the file is saved, or at regular intervals.

Alternatively, copies of the shared spreadsheet can be sent out to different users. Each user updates their copy then returns it. The returned copies can then be merged together, with all the changes being either accepted or ignored.

Manoeuvres

1. Open the supplied workbook **Hotel**. This workbook is to be shared. Save the workbook as **Communal**.

2. To allow the workbook to be shared, on the **Review** tab, in the **Changes** group, click **Share Workbook**. Click the **Editing** tab.

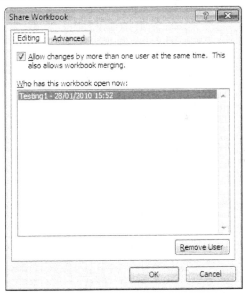

3. Click in the **Allow changes** option box, to activate it. Click the **Advanced** tab to see the available settings.

4. Click **OK**. *Excel* will need to save the workbook with its new status and a message is displayed. Click **OK**. The workbook is saved as shared, and the **Title Bar** of the window will now show the word **Shared** next to the file name.

continued over

Driving Lesson 95 - Continued

5.   If the file is saved in an accessible location, e.g. on a server, any other user can now open and amend any part of the file (unless it is protected) while it is still open on your computer.

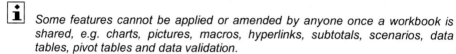 *Some features cannot be applied or amended by anyone once a workbook is shared, e.g. charts, pictures, macros, hyperlinks, subtotals, scenarios, data tables, pivot tables and data validation.*

6.   To see who has a shared file open, select **Share Workbook** on the **Review** tab. Click the **Editing** tab.

This picture shows 2 users accessing the workbook.

7.   Click **OK**. When another user changes data in the workbook, you will be notified and see the updates when you save your copy.

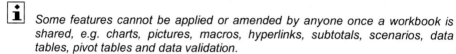 *By changing settings in the **Advanced** view of the **Share Workbook** dialog box, the updates can be applied automatically and regularly.*

8.   Close the workbook **Communal**.

Driving Lesson 96 - Merging Workbooks

P Park and Read

Another way to share workbooks is to send copies out to various users so they can make their own amendments. The copies can then be merged back together, with the original user deciding which amendments to accept or ignore.

Manoeuvres

1.   Open the supplied workbook **Bookings** and then save it as **Holiday**. This workbook is to be sent out for review but first it must be shared.

2.   Select **Share Workbook** on the **Review** tab and click in the **Allow changes** option box in the **Editing** view.

3.   Click the **Advanced** tab and change the history to 14 days. This means changes can be kept for up to 14 days and still be merged.

4.   Click **OK** to share the workbook and **OK** again. Now the workbook can be sent out.

5.   One way to send out the file is to email it. Click the **File** tab then **Save & Send**. With **Send Using E-mail** selected click **Send as Attachment**. Your mail application will open with the workbook attached ready to send, add the message **Please review the attached workbook**.

6.   Address the message to another user and send it.

ℹ️ *Any method of sending out the workbook can be used, such as copying over a network or writing to a floppy disk or CD.*

7.   Open the workbook at its destination and make some small changes, e.g. change the value in cell **C12** from **4** to **2**.

8.   Save the amended workbook with a different name, e.g. **Holiday1**, and send it back to its original user. Make sure it is saved in the same location as the original, **Holiday**.

ℹ️ *The **Compare and Merge Workbooks** command is not displayed by default in Excel 2010. To add it to the **Quick Access Toolbar**, right click on the **File** tab and select **Customize Quick Access Toolbar** from the options. From the **Choose commands from** list select **All Commands**. From the list of commands in the category, select **Compare and Merge Workbooks**, click **Add**, and then **OK**.*

continued over

Driving Lesson 96 - Continued

9. With the original **Holiday** file open, select **Compare and Merge Workbooks**, , from the **Quick Access Toolbar**.

10. Select the returned file (**Holiday1**) from the **Select Files** dialog box and click **OK**.

11. To review the changes, display the **Review** tab and click **Track Changes** then **Accept/Reject Changes**.

12. Leave the settings as shown and click **OK**. A dialog box will appear for each change in turn.

13. Each change can be accepted or rejected. If rejected, the original value will remain. Click **Accept**. When there are no more dialog boxes, all changes have been reviewed.

14. To remove the workbook from shared use, on the **Review** tab, click **Share Workbook**.

15. Uncheck the **Allow changes** option and click **OK**. Click **Yes** at the confirmation prompt.

16. Close the workbook **Holiday**.

Driving Lesson 97 - Revision: Tracking

This is not an ECDL test. Testing may only be carried out through certified ECDL test centres. This covers the features introduced in this section. Try not to refer to the preceding Driving Lessons while completing it.

1. Open the workbook **Draft**. As the managing director of the company, you want to allow your factory manager to amend the budget predictions you have created.

2. Save the workbook as **Draft1**.

3. Set the workbook up so that it can be amended by other users while you still have it open and save it.

 For the benefit of people without network facilities, the updates in this exercise will actually be made <u>without</u> sharing.

4. Close the workbook.

5. Now take the part of the factory manager. Open the **Draft1** workbook.

6. You need extra workers in the summer to cover for holidays. Change the **Workers** value for **June**, **July** and **August** to **25**.

7. The canteen roof is leaking. Insert a new row above **Overheads**. Enter a label of **Repairs** and a value of **£4000** in **January**.

8. Change the **Overheads** figure for **April** to **£6000** to cover the annual golf competition. Save the workbook and close it.

9. You are now the MD again. Open the **Draft1** workbook to review your manager's changes.

10. Start the **Accept or Reject Changes** process. According to the dialog box, how many changes have been made?

11. Work through the changes, accepting the extra worker details and the overheads for the golf, but rejecting the repairs to the canteen (reject the insertion of the new row, and all associated changes will be lost).

12. You are feeling generous; add **£20** to the **Overheads** figure in **January** to buy new buckets for the canteen. What is the final **Total Net Profit** figure?

13. Remove the workbook from shared use, save it as **Draft1** and close it.

 *Answers are shown in the **Answers** section at the end of the guide.*

If you experienced any difficulty completing this Revision refer back to the Driving Lessons in this section. Then redo the Revision.

Once you are confident with the features, complete the Record of Achievement Matrix referring to the Section at the end of the guide.

Answers

Driving Lesson 3

Step 1   It is easier to manage, different people can perform different tasks, people working on one part will not have access to the rest.

Step 2   So that any scrolling will only be in one direction. This makes a spreadsheet, easier to use, easier to understand and easier to print.

Step 3   Protecting the contents of cells that do not need to be changed stops them from being deleted, even accidentally. Sensitive data can also be password protected to stop unwanted viewing.

Step 4   You may need to produce a user guide, or provide training or act as a help desk.

Step 5   **Lists** (prices, materials, customers, range of units). **Linking** (displaying prices on a calculation sheet - orders). **Formulas** and **Functions** (to perform any calculations). **Formatting** (easier to use, pleasant for customers to see, good clear printouts etc.). **Analysis** (sales figures, stock used, profit, turnover, accounts etc). **Charts** (to represent figures). Plus any other item from page 11, depending on how you approach the task.

Step 6   A **template** is a base spreadsheet with all formatting and calculations included ready for data to be added. They are used repeatedly for consistency.

Step 7   A **macro** is a method performing repetitive tasks with one action.

Step 8   As a **chart**, either: on paper, as a web page on the Internet, on a slide for a presentation.

Step 9   A **link** gets and displays information from another source, a **hyperlink** takes you to another source when clicked.

Driving Lesson 25

Step 5   **=Sum((Food February):(Advertising February))**

Step 8   **Yes, £4362.92**

Step 10 **=Function_Rooms December**

Driving Lesson 34

Step 2   The **IF** statement entered into cell **J4** should be **=IF(I4=0,0,(H4-I4)/I4)**. This should then be replicated down the column as far as cell J10. There are 5 cells in the workbook that contain incorrect ranges in functions: The correct range for the function in cell **H8** is **C8:G8**. The correct range for the function in cell **D10** is **D4:D9**. The correct range for the function in cell **E10** is **E4:E9**. The correct range for the function in cell **H10** is **H4:H9**. The correct range for the function in cell **K10** is **K4:K9**.

Driving Lesson 48

Step 4   The formula to calculate % occupancy would be =rooms/300.

Step 10 The completed chart.

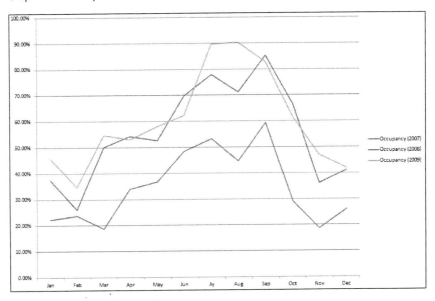

Driving Lesson 50

Step 16 The second cheapest car is the **Austin Mini**.

Step 17 The car with the most mileage is the **Fiat 126**.

Driving Lesson 60

Step 2   There are 3 members of staff in the Computer Services department.

Step 4   There are 8 members of staff aged between 40 and 50 years inclusive.

Step 8   3 records should have been extracted.

Driving Lesson 64

Step 3   The created Pivot Table.

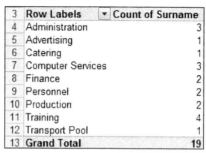

Row Labels ▼	Count of Surname
4	Administration	3
5	Advertising	1
6	Catering	1
7	Computer Services	3
8	Finance	2
9	Personnel	2
10	Production	2
11	Training	4
12	Transport Pool	1
13	Grand Total	19

This solution excludes the personal details you entered

Step 8   The age group with the most absences is the **Over 50s**.

Driving Lesson 70

Step 12 =MID(A15,9,2)&"/"&MID(A15,7,2)&"/"&MID(A15,6,1)&MID(A15,11,1)

Step 13 The date of birth is 28/10/57

Driving Lesson 71

Step 12 The monthly repayment is £299.78

Step 13 The repayments rise to £366.88

Step 16 The maximum amount that can be borrowed is £40,885.05

Step 17 The result should be £447,107.83

Driving Lesson 72

Step 9   There should be a total of 75 replies.

Step 10 The oldest person to reply is 97 years old.

Step 11 The youngest person to reply is 24 years old.

Step 12 The total age of all respondents should be more than 3550.

Step 13 The average age of all respondents should be more than 47.

Note: This workbook uses dates of birth and as a result the answers increase over time. At release these answers were correct.

Driving Lesson 73

Step 8   8 employees qualify for the bonus.

Driving Lesson 74

Step 2   The formula is **=COUNTIF(E5,E24>=40)**. Answer **15**.

Step 3   The formula is **=DOUNT(A5:F24,E5,A1:F2)**. **15**.

Step 4   The formula is **=DAVERAGE(A5:F24,E5,A1:F2)**.Answer **51+**

Step 5   The formula is **=ROUND(F28,0)**. Answer **52**.

Step 6   Change cell **E2** to **>=30**. The answers are **18** and **49**.

Step 7   **=HLOOKUP(F6,$B$31:$E$32,2)** where the lookup is placed at B31:E32 in this instance.

Step 8   **=IF(OR(D6="Finance",D6="Training"),100,20)**.

Step 9   **=YEAR(C6)+65** formatted as a whole number.

Step 10   **=CONCATENATE(B6," ",A6)**

Note that the answers for Steps 2 to 6 are continually increasing due to the NOW() function and therefore are only provided as a guide.

Driving Lesson 82

Step 9   7 rooms

Step 11 Yes, profit of £20 rather than loss of £30.

Driving Lesson 93

Step 4   The Precedents of cell **H8** are cells **F8** and **G8**.

Step 5   The Dependents of cell **F11** are cells **G11** and **H11**.

Step 6   The Precedents of cell **D13** are cell **E13** and the list starting at **K5**.

Driving Lesson 97

Step 10 **7** changes have been made

Step 12 The total Net Profit is now **9108**

Glossary

Auditing	Allows relationships between formulas and their component cells/ranges to be displayed.
AVERAGE	A function that adds the values in a range of cells, then divides the result by the number of values added.
Comment	Text that is attached to a cell as a background note. Displayed when the pointer is placed over the appropriate cell.
Concatenate	A function that can be used to combine the contents of two or more cells that contain text.
Container	A document that contains a link to a cell or range in a source document. If data in the source is modified, the container will automatically be updated.
COUNT	A function that will display the number of numerical values in a range of cells.
Data Table	Used to see how changing one variable in a formula affects its result over a range of values.
Data Validation	Check for correctness of data that is entered into cells.
Database Function	A function that is specifically designed to be used with lists.
Dependent	A cell that is referenced in a formula.
Delimited Text	Data within a text file, where the text is separated by commas, tabs, etc. This type of data may be imported into a worksheet.
Error	A message that is displayed when a formula cannot be calculated. The nature of the message identifies the reason for the error.
Field	A cell on a row within a list.
Field Name	The heading at the top of a column of fields within a list.
Filter	A tool that matches records in a list to specified criteria.
Format as Table	Applies a set of pre-defined formatting to a worksheet in order to enhance its appearance.
Formula	A calculation, can use values and/or cell references.
Function	A specialised formula that makes calculations easier.
Go To	A command that can be used to navigate to a cell or range by using its reference or name.

Link	A formula reference to a cell or range in another location within the same worksheet, or another worksheet either in the same or a different workbook. A link allows data edited in the source worksheet to automatically update in the container worksheet. Links may be created to other file types.
List	A labelled series of rows that separates information into columns, each containing similar information.
Lookup	A function that looks up relevant data from a table, and uses it in a calculation.
Macro	A recorded sequence of commands that can be replayed as required in order to automate routine tasks.
Name	Cell or range references may be replaced by names to simplify navigation around a worksheet or understanding of formulae.
Nested Function	A combination of individual functions combined with each other to perform more complex calculations.
Outlines	An outline creates a view that can show different amounts of data. The levels are **displayed** or **hidden** to show the data required by the user.
PivotTable	A table that organises and summarises large amounts of data from within a range of labelled columns. The fields within a PivotTable may be moved (Pivoted) around between the axes and data area to analyse the data in various ways.
Precedent	A cell that is referenced by a formula.
Protection	Passwords may be used to set various levels of security for cells, worksheets or workbooks
Record	A completed row of information within a list.
Scenario	A specific combination of values and solutions that has been named and saved within a worksheet. This can then be compared to other combinations.
Source Document	A worksheet containing data that is linked to a cell or range in a container worksheet. If this data is changed, the linked cell or range will automatically be updated.
SubTotal	A function that can be applied to a list to display SUM, COUNT, or AVERAGE for each group with a grand total for the whole list.
SUM	A function that will add the values in a range of cells.
Template	A base worksheet that provides a layout ready for data to be entered.

Index

Record of Achievement Matrix

This Matrix is to be used to measure your progress while working through the guide. This is a learning reinforcement process, you judge when you are competent.

Tick boxes are provided for each feature. 1 is for no knowledge, 2 some knowledge and 3 is for competent. A section is only complete when column 3 is completed for all parts of the section.

For details on sitting ECDL Examinations in your country please contact the local ECDL Licensee or visit the European Computer Driving Licence Foundation Limited web site at http://www.ecdl.org.

Tick the Relevant Boxes **1**: No Knowledge **2**: Some Knowledge **3**: Competent

Section	No	Driving Lesson	1	2	3
1 Introduction	1	Spreadsheet Design			
	2	Techniques to Use			
2 Formatting	4	Split a Window			
	5	Conditional Formatting			
	6	Format as Table			
	7	Paste Special			
	8	Transposing Data			
	9	Copying and Moving Sheets			
3 Protection	11	Protection			
	12	Worksheet and Cell Protection			
	13	Hiding Rows and Columns			
	14	Hiding Formulas			
	15	Workbook Protection			
	16	Hiding Worksheets and Workbooks			
4 Cell Comments	18	Cell Comments			
	19	Display Comments			
	20	Create, Edit & Delete Comments			
5 Names	22	Names			
	23	Using Names in Formulas			
	24	Using Go To with Names			
6 Templates	26	Creating a Template			
	27	Using a Template			
	28	Editing a Template			
7 Formulas	30	Displaying Formulas			
	31	Formulas that Produce Errors			
	32	Mixed Referencing			
	33	Custom Number Formats			

Tick the Relevant Boxes **1**: No Knowledge **2**: Some Knowledge **3**: Competent

Section	No	Driving Lesson	1	2	3
8 Outlines	35	Creating an Outline			
	36	Working with an Outline			
9 Scenarios	38	Creating Scenarios			
	39	Using and Editing Scenarios			
	40	Scenario Summary Reports			
10 Linking & Importing	42	Linking			
	43	Creating Links			
	44	Linking between Workbooks			
	45	Linking to a Word Document			
	46	Hyperlinks			
	47	Importing Delimited Data			
11 Sorting	49	Sorting			
	50	Multiple Column Sorts			
	51	Custom Lists and Sorts			
12 Lists	53	Lists			
	54	Filtering Lists			
	55	AutoFilter			
	56	Custom AutoFilter			
	57	Advanced Filtering			
	58	Extracting Filtered Data			
	59	Adding Subtotals			
13 Pivot Tables	61	PivotTables			
	62	Filtering a PivotTable			
	63	Grouping and Sorting in PivotTables			

Tick the Relevant Boxes **1**: No Knowledge **2**: Some Knowledge **3**: Competent

Section	No	Driving Lesson	1	2	3
14 Functions	65	Functions			
	66	Date and Time Functions			
	67	Lookup Functions			
	68	Mathematical Functions			
	69	Statistical Functions			
	70	Text Functions			
	71	Financial Functions			
	72	Database Functions			
	73	Nested Functions			
15 Charts	75	Formatting Charts			
	76	Modifying Charts			
	77	Line-Column Charts			
	78	Adding Images to Charts			
16 Data Tables	80	One Input Data Table			
	81	Two Input Data Table			
17 Macros	83	Macros			
	84	Recording a Macro			
	85	Running a Macro			
	86	Assigning a Macro to the Quick Access Toolbar			
18 Auditing	88	Auditing			
	89	Tracing Precedents			
	90	Tracing Dependents			
	91	Tracing Errors			
	92	Data Validation			
19 Tracking Changes	94	Track Changes in a Worksheet			
	95	Shared Workbooks			
	96	Merging Workbooks			

Other Products from CiA Training

CiA Training is a leading publishing company which has consistently delivered the highest quality products since 1985. Our experienced in-house publishing team has developed a wide range of flexible and easy to use self-teach resources for individual learners and corporate clients all over the world.

At the time of publication, we currently offer approved ECDL materials for:

- **ECDL Syllabus 5.0**

- **ECDL Syllabus 5.0 Revision Series**

- **ECDL Advanced Syllabus 2.0**

- **ECDL Advanced Syllabus 2.0 Revision Series**

Previous syllabus versions are also available upon request.

We hope you have enjoyed using this guide and would love to hear your opinions about our materials. To let us know how we're doing, and to get up to the minute information on our current range of products, please visit us at:

www.ciatraining.co.uk